HOW TO MAKE MONEY PUBLISHING FROM HOME

Everything You Need to Know
to Successfully Publish:
Books, Newsletters, Greeting Cards,
Zines, and Software

Lisa Shaw

PRIMA PUBLISHING

For all of my home-based publishing buddies
who just laugh at it all sometimes. . . .

© 1997 by Lisa Shaw

Prima Publishing and colophon are registered trademarks of Prima Communications, Inc.

Library of Congress Cataloging-in-Publication Data
Shaw, Lisa Angowski Rogak.
How to make money publishing from home: everything you need to know to successfully publish: books, newsletters, greeting cards, zines, and software / Lisa Shaw.
    p.   cm.
Includes index.
ISBN 0-7615-0812-0
1. Publishers and publishing—United States—Management. 2. Home-based businesses—United States—Management. 3. Desktop publishing industry—United States—Management. I. Title.
Z471.S445 1997
070.5'068—dc21
                                          97-18930
                                          CIP

99 00 01 HH 10 9 8 7 6 5 4 3 2

Printed in the United States of America

HOW TO ORDER
Single copies may be ordered from Prima Publishing, P.O. Box 1260BK, Rocklin, CA 95677; telephone (916) 632-4400. Quantity discounts are also available. On your letterhead, include information concerning the intended use of the books and the number of books you wish to purchase.

Visit us online at http://www.primapublishing.com

Contents

Part 3 The Business of Running Your Home-Based Publishing Business

Introduction

For the most part, I've always worked for myself, running my own publishing business out of my home since 1981. It hasn't always been easy, especially in the days before the first crude desktop publishing software programs became available, but I've always preferred to work for myself than to work for someone else. Whether publishing newsletters, writing books, producing computer software, or creating and selling a line of greeting cards, I've done well in part because I've been able to call the shots as to what I produce, where I work, and how I work. For me, that means that I can live in a rural area, work at home surrounded by my six cats, and let voice mail pick up whenever I'm feeling particularly anti-social.

In the past, whenever I've accepted a regular job—that is, working in an office for somebody else—my tenure was inevitably short. I either got fired or quit after a month or two. Rather than having a regular paycheck, I have preferred to rely on my own efforts and be poor but free. I've managed to stick it out long enough that I am making some money and I'm still free—to a certain extent.

In the sixteen years that I've been running my own home-based publishing business, I've run into a lot of people who don't understand why I do what I do. And once *you* start your own business, there's a good chance that you'll run into the same kind of people, those who would rather give up their freedom and creativity in order to possess that elusive thing known as "security" as well as some degree of status within that field. More often than not, they resent people like you and me, those who are willing to take the chance to be happy with their work.

Yes, money—or the lack of it—also enters into the equation, but you'll quickly discover that you need more than money to get a home-based publishing business off the ground and keep it growing. Having adequate money to start and run your business can actually be a handicap because it's an easy trap to rely on dollars first and effort second. In fact, I had no money in my early publishing ventures, so I had to rely solely on my creativity and my intractable faith in my own abilities. In other words, I'm stubborn and independent to a fault: If I wanted to make something happen, I couldn't wait around for someone else to do it because *it wasn't gonna happen.*

Regardless of the type of publishing business you're thinking about starting, this book will provide you with lots of information on financing, business planning, marketing, and legal and tax issues along with the day-to-day considerations of running a business. And, of course, I include lots of ideas about specific types of home-based publishing businesses.

So start dreaming about the type of home-based publishing business you'd like to run.

PART ONE

The Home-Based Publishing Industry

1

Why Run a Home-Based Publishing Business Now?

These days it seems that trends come from out of nowhere and garner a lot of press coverage overnight. All eyes turn toward whatever happens to be hot at the moment, from new concepts in the business world to expensive sports cars that look like throat lozenges. Such fads are usually very popular for a short time, then either quickly fade into the background or disappear entirely as their primary appeal wears off.

On the surface, that's how it appears to be with a home-based publishing business. "Yeah," you may think, "it's great to work at home, publish anything you want, and make some money besides, but you just wait and see, it'll never catch on." Such perceptions are understandable but probably inaccurate. Though running your own home-based publishing business is a radical departure from the traditional corporate structure Americans have slavishly followed for the last one hundred years—and have only recently begun to abandon in significant numbers—all the signs suggest that this new form of independent publishing will catch on permanently.

The advent and quick development of high technology and the seemingly magical things you can do with computers today (machines that are a tiny fraction of the size and price of the computers of twenty years ago) have been largely responsible for the growing popularity of home-based publishing businesses. Even though a new computer is nearly obsolete the minute you carry it out of the computer store, the developing power of today's and tomorrow's computers will allow people to work more effectively, more quickly, and to live and run their publishing businesses anywhere, even out of a tepee, if they want.

The Internet and the World Wide Web, along with e-mail, fax machines, and overnight delivery services, have brought the world closer to us. Instead of having to leave home and slog through stacks of books, journals, and periodicals to find information, we can now conduct research anytime of the day or night from home. It's been a year since I renewed my library card at Dartmouth College, a thirty-five-mile trek from my house. There's no need to, because I can find everything by logging onto the Internet.

Yes, even today there are some people who still regard working and running a business from home as a radical concept. But the U.S. economy has long been in the process of converting itself from a manufacturing base to one that values information. This means that entrepreneurs who are able to provide people with the information they're looking for—in the form of a book, newsletter, computer disk, or in another form—will have no trouble succeeding. But it still requires lots of hard work, creative marketing, superb customer service, and a little bit of luck and timing.

Home-Based Publishing: A Growing Trend

Running a home-based publishing business is catching on across the country for a number of reasons.

Futurist Alvin Toffler, author of *Future Shock* and *The Third Wave,* has spent years telling Americans that millions of us would work at home in what he dubbed "electronic cottages." His prediction that information would become the currency that drives the American economy is coming true. But his prediction that massive urban office buildings would stand empty amidst formerly bustling downtowns hasn't come to pass—*yet*.

Long commutes to an outside office consume time and energy, and make people less productive not only at work but at home, too. Additional time is usually required each day and on the weekend to decompress from the stresses of the week. Running your own publishing business from your home eliminates some, if not all, of this kind of stress. And, of course, being your own boss has become the dream of millions of Americans.

Here are some other benefits:

- Rural residents are starting their own home-based publishing businesses in increasing numbers because they can earn more money that way than working in their local economy. By working for themselves and focusing on a national market, people who run home-based publishing businesses not only can earn a decent living but may also stimulate economies in regions that are traditionally depressed.
- People desire to pursue other interests—hobbies, part-time and/or seasonal businesses, even education. In other words, they want to do more than just spend all of their waking hours at work. Running a home-based publishing business can save wasted hours in the day by eliminating the time spent traveling to an outside office. The time saved can be spent on these outside pursuits, or with friends and family.
- And finally, people who run home-based publishing businesses can save money because they're not spending lots of dollars on lunches out, tolls, gas, parking, and appropriate business attire.

Why Are People More Interested in Running a Home-Based Publishing Business?

When asked if they would like to start their own home-based publishing business, people who love to read and who also love the written word usually respond enthusiastically. Their minds start racing with thoughts of being their own boss, producing their own literature, and having an audience of avid readers who are eager to hear their opinions and ideas. But usually their enthusiasm soon wanes. After the initial rush of dreaming about running their own businesses, they immediately start thinking of all of the reasons why they won't be able to pull it off.

The fact is that today more people are thinking about starting their own home-based publishing business and here's why:

- *The desire to accomplish what you want to do for a change.* Several generations of Americans—baby boomers and generation X'ers—have been unfairly branded by the media as selfish. The truth is that many people—especially women—are more selfless than they made out to be. Here, too, people seek balance: In order to give to others, one has to give to oneself as well. And following your dreams by working from home and running your own publishing business is a great way to start.

- *The desire to break through the glass ceiling or rise above the sticky floor.* If you haven't already made it to where you think you should be by now in your current field or job, then your chances of ever reaching the upper echelons of your company or industry probably aren't that great— unless you start doing things differently. This is often the point when people start to investigate the possibility of starting their own business, and a publishing one at that, if they've long wanted to impart information to the world.

- *The desire to explore a particular interest in depth.* When you're young and idealistic, it's easy to envision reaching your career goals by the age of twenty-five. In most cases, of course, real life intercedes, and the need to make a living pushes your main focus to the back burner, where it remains until retirement, if it manages to resurface at all. But sometimes, everyday life—the job, the family, the bills—just becomes too much to bear, and you figure, "Dammit, I work hard, why shouldn't I be able to do what

I want?" By working from home and running your own publishing business, you'll be able to explore your own interests and make money at it besides.

- *Refusal to buy into the corporate structure.* Millions of baby boomers poured into the mainstream labor markets in the 1970s and 1980s. Some immediately saw all the warts and left; most decided to stick it out. But when things didn't get much better, they decided to take matters into their own hands by starting their own businesses from their home offices, where they could get their work done in peace and quiet, and avoid the constant onslaught of office politics that seems to consume so much of the typical employee's day.

Probably at least one of your reasons for wanting to start your own home-based publishing business is listed above. Some of you might agree with every item on the list, yet remain convinced that the best thing to do is to suffer in silence—you need your job and you don't want to lose that security, the economy's tight, and. . . .

Don't think like this. Once you declare your intention to start your own home-based publishing business, you're well on the way. You'll also be calling your own shots and will eventually start to make more money than you ever could by hanging onto a steady job with a steady paycheck. However, don't be surprised if you receive some negative reactions from family and friends who may also want to start their own businesses but haven't done it yet. There's a good chance that if they see you go ahead with pursuing your dreams, they'll view you as disturbing the status quo. "What makes you think you're better than the rest of us?" they may ask—that is, if they even have the guts to bring it up with you. "Why do you think you have what it takes to do what you want if the rest of us can't?"

But the fact is, you're not like the rest; by picking up a copy of this book, you're beginning to take the necessary steps to live the kind of life that you really want to live.

The Benefits of Running Your Own Home-Based Publishing Business

Here are some of the advantages that you will enjoy by starting your own home-based publishing business:

- Less commuting time, more time to work and play.
- More time for yourself and your family.
- More time for leisure pursuits.
- Less stress, better health.
- Less money spent on gas, clothes, and meals out.

The Disadvantages of Running a Home-Based Publishing Business

Of course, even though working from home is wonderful in many ways, there are a few disadvantages, and it's not for everyone. Even the most content home-based publishers admit to some downsides of working out of their homes:

- You may feel isolated if you work by yourself.
- You may find it difficult to motivate yourself.
- You may find that it's hard to stop working at the end of the day.
- Your neighbors may drop in to socialize, and you may find it hard to turn them away.
- It may be hard to resist the refrigerator, TV, or other distractions in your home.
- It may take awhile until the business starts to generate revenue.

With a little effort, as well as an awareness of the disadvantages of home-based publishing, you'll be well armed to deal with them when they do arise.

2

Taking Stock of Your Home-Based Publishing Business

If you want to start your own home-based publishing business, the first thing you should know is that you probably already possess all the skills that you'll need to be a success. You'll just need to do a bit of homework first.

Start by figuring out the reasons why you want to run your own publishing business, as well as being realistic in your expectations about how difficult it will be.

A Day in the Life of a Home-Based Publishing Business

I'll tell you right now, the best thing about running your own home-based publishing business is that every day is different. You won't even have time to watch the clock.

What's the worst thing about it?

Surprise! It's the same thing—the fact that every day is different. How you handle this simple fact depends on the type of person you are. If you thrive on order and predictability, you may not be comfortable running your own home-based publishing business, especially in the beginning when you will probably be doing everything yourself, from writing copy, making sales calls, buying office supplies, and stuffing envelopes.

I once drew up a schedule of a typical day when I was publishing two newsletters at the same time: *Travel Marketing Bulletin,* a marketing newsletter for small travel businesses (which I have since discontinued), and *Sticks,* a newsletter for people who want to move to the country (which I have since sold). Now I'm publishing books and greeting cards in addition to updating a computer program that I originally developed and marketed in 1995. Through trial and error I've learned two important things: how to delegate more of my work to outside businesses and independent contractors, and how to schedule more time where I do nothing in order to compensate for my breakneck work pace. What follows is a fairly typical day when I was publishing these two newsletters, which of course means that it was anything *but* typical.

A "Typical" 8:00–5:00 Work Schedule

8:00 A.M   The phone rings on my 800 line. It's a man on the West Coast who's up early and wants to subscribe to *Sticks* with his MasterCard. I write down the information and fill out an order form, a credit card slip, address an envelope and put the current issue inside, and add his name and address to my computerized database and subscription list. This scenario will be repeated at least five more times that day with this newsletter, and three times for *Travel Marketing Bulletin.* I'll also receive calls from an average of fifteen people a day who want information on each newsletter. For each of them, I'll again address an envelope, put a brochure in it, place a stamp on the envelope, and add their name to the prospect file on my computer.

8:30 A.M.   I review my list of what needs to be done that day, which includes a mailing to fifty radio show producers, phoning a couple of my freelance writers to talk about article ideas for the upcoming issues, calling the printer to order 500 more copies of my new brochure, and researching a couple of stories for one of the newsletters. Of course, with all the phone calls and the onslaught of mail that must be dealt with every day, I'll be lucky if I'm able to cross off half of the items on my list. I start printing out the cover letters for the media mailing on my laser printer.

9:20 A.M.   The phone rings. It's an account executive from a New York public relations firm wanting to know if I'll run a story on her client in *Travel Marketing Bulletin*. I told her that it doesn't seem likely, given the fact that neither she nor her client has ever seen a copy of the newsletter.

9:45 A.M.   A writer sends her article—three days late—over the fax. I usually have writers send their stories in on disk to save typing time on my end, not to mention my wrists. Because this article was faxed I must stop what I'm doing and start typing the story directly into the newsletter layout. As soon as I'm finished, I can send the completed camera-ready newsletter through my modem to my printer. In the past, I've had to drive it there myself.

10:05 A.M.   A man in Milwaukee calls to get a sample copy of *Sticks* after he read about it in his local paper.

10:20 A.M.   A subscriber calls to order a copy of a new book on marketing I've just begun to sell through *Travel Marketing Bulletin*. Because I don't like to tie up money or storage space in keeping my own inventory of books, each such order must be forwarded to the publisher. After I finish taking the order, I call my sales rep at the publisher, who sends me out a copy the same day, along with a bill.

10:30 A.M.   I go back to typing the late article into the computer.

10:32 A.M.   The phone rings. It's a radio producer who wants to set up a live phone interview with me the day after tomorrow. I prepare a mailing label and call an express mail company to come pick up the package of materials the producer and the host need to review before the show.

10:45 A.M.   I return to the computer.

11:15 A.M.   I finish typing in the late article and do some light editing on it. I press a couple of buttons and a few seconds later it's in my printer's computer. A few days later I will send my updated mailing list to him the same way—he also stuffs the envelopes and sends the newsletter out—so that people who have become new subscribers since the last issue will be added to the printer's master list.

11:25 A.M.   I go back to printing out letters for the press mailing. I finish the letters and start sifting through the mail, which has just arrived.

11:43 A.M.   It seems that one of the subscription checks I deposited last week bounced. I subtract the amount from my checking account, remove the name from the subscription list, and call up the computer file that contains the letter I regularly send to deadbeats like this one. After I tack on a $20 handling fee—the amount my bank charges me plus $5 for me for the hassle—I usually don't hear from the subscriber again. Either they're too embarrassed or they think it's too expensive. Most often, I end up writing the bank fee off as a tax deductible business expense. I don't mind this as much as the fact that it's interrupted the flow of my day.

12:15 P.M.   I turn the answering machine on and leave the office for an hour. Without this break each day, I'd be cranky and tired by midafternoon.

1:30 P.M.   Back in the office with five messages on the answering machine, all from people who want more information about the newsletters. They always call during lunchtime, I figure, so I can call back on my dime, even when they call on the 800 line.

1:55 P.M.   Fifty press kits to stuff and mail by 4:00, and I've only finished the cover letters. I still have to staple press releases, select which sample copies and press clips I'm going to enclose, put it all in the folder, stuff and stamp the envelope, and put the address labels on the envelopes, all in the next two hours. It may not sound like much, but this is why answering machines were invented. I resolve to ignore the phone—or at least screen my messages—so I can finish this job, which is already a few days late.

3:55 P.M.   I make it to the post office as the mail pickup truck pulls in ahead of me. My mailing makes it out today with minutes to spare.

4:10 P.M.   Back in the office. Four people have called since I've been gone. It's not just that people wait until lunch to call, I'm convinced they sense when I'm out of the office. Some days I love the phone, other days I hate it. I proceed to return all the calls.

4:40 P.M.   I discover I didn't call any of the people on my list for today. That means they go to the top of the list for tomorrow. I make another To Do list.

4:50 P.M.   The phone rings. It's a subscriber who wants to write an article for the next issue.

5:10 P.M.   We hang up, with me encouraging the subscriber to restrict his topic, making it more narrow. While I've been on the phone, two more calls have come in, which were forwarded to my fax line that is also an answering machine. I return the calls.

5:30 P.M.   I start to close up the office for the day, but like always I realize that I could easily spend another ten hours here and not get everything done that I need to do. This is one reason why I do most of my writing in the evening or on the weekends, when the phone doesn't ring as much and my concentration is better.

Income and Profit Potentials

As is the case with any new business, in the beginning it may seem as though you're working for free, as you pour every penny of revenue back into your home-based publishing business, whether it's for a new computer system and more advanced software or more brochures or copy paper.

Don't worry. Most new home-based publishing entrepreneurs find themselves in this dilemma. In the beginning it's unlikely that you'll have to invest huge amounts of cash up front or tie up a significant amount of money in overhead or inventory like other businesses. If you work hard at keeping your expenses down (with inexpensive marketing techniques) while increasing your revenue, in time you'll be able to afford to farm out more work and pay yourself a salary as well.

The amount of money you'll be able to make from your business depends on how much marketing you'll do, how big your market is, and where you'll later choose to branch out, whether it's by offering more specialized services to your customers or expanding your customer base.

Of course, hiring an employee or subcontracting some of the work out to other businesses will increase your expenses. But at the same time, it will free up some of your time so that you can concentrate your energy on tasks that will bring in more business and more revenue, if indeed that is what you would like to focus on. If you can, leave the grunt work—or the work that you don't like to do—to someone else, whether it's a mailing house or an employee for sorting and stuffing your bulk mailings.

Risk Potential

Anyone who starts a publishing business from their home will face a certain amount of risk. Though statistics say that 90 percent of new businesses won't make it to see their fifth anniversaries, the survival rate for home-based publishing businesses that start with little or no capital, ironically, is much healthier.

One problem that frequently occurs when people invest money in a small business is that they want to feel like they're running a real business, and not be relegated to running their operations from a corner of the kitchen table. And even though they may not have any clients or business lined up, publishing entrepreneurs sometimes fall into the trap of spending thousands of dollars on fancy office furniture, rent, and complicated phone systems for their home offices. Two years later, they're nowhere to be seen, their business phone lines long ago disconnected. Why? Because they thought it was more important to assume the trappings of successful entrepreneurs, those who have been in business for awhile and have earned enough money to furnish their offices, instead of plowing all their income back into the business so that they could generate more business and more revenue.

Your chances for making it to your fifth anniversary are much improved if the focus of your business is suitably narrow, if you've determined that your audience is large enough, and if you provide a product or publication that reaches an audience that is not being adequately served.

Look in the obvious places to find your competition: in your town and region, in industry publications, and at associations. Try to get an idea of the way they run their businesses to see what's good and what's bad about it. What are they not doing that you think they should? Use this information to define the theme of your own business, publications, and products in a different way to increase your chances of success in the field. The good news is that if you find several competitors who cover the same ground that you plan to, the audience is probably large enough to support one more business.

Assessing Your Personal Goals

Before you proceed to run headlong into running your own home-based publishing business, it's a good idea to take some time to evaluate yourself, your financial situation, and the skills you'll need to succeed. Doing your homework at this stage will save you from making big and possibly costly mistakes down the road.

First, you must determine what your overall personal goals are and how running your own home-based publishing business fits in with them—and vice versa.

Take some time to answer the following questions in detail:

- What are the three main reasons why you want to run your own home-based publishing business?
- How long do you plan to run your business?
- Do you view your business as a part- or a full-time endeavor?
- What are your personal goals aside from running your business? Do you plan to retire at a certain age, or move on to something else after running the business?

As you've already surmised, the fantasy of freedom that's implied in running your own business does not even begin to match the reality—even though you probably won't fully admit to this until you're knee-deep in the business. But many home-based publishing entrepreneurs view their business as a means to an end: It provides a way to have some control over their lives, or it may provide a way to live where they want to while making a decent living. The safe alternative may be a job where you're doing most of the work for a paltry salary while your boss is just sitting back and depositing his checks in the bank. If you were in charge of running your own home-based publishing business, you'd still be busting your butt, but at least you'd be getting paid fairly for it.

Running your own home-based publishing business is like any other job: You need it to provide income along with a healthy dose of satisfaction. But you also need to have something in your life besides the business. That's why it's important to set goals for yourself that are totally separate from the business. Burnout is very common when you run your own business, whether or not you run it from your home or you're in the publishing field. One way to prevent burnout is to carefully plan in advance all of your personal goals—that is, goals that have absolutely nothing to do with your business—whether you want to learn a foreign language or spend more time with your friends and family. If you run a business, setting goals is very necessary.

Assessing Your Financial Goals

If you want to get rich, go and buy a book that tells you how—but you'll still have to buy an occasional lottery ticket. If you want to have a decent income while you build equity and increase your revenues a little bit each year, then keep reading. You're on the right track in wanting to start your own home-based publishing business.

To see if your financial goals jibe with the goal of running your own publishing business from home, ask yourself the following questions:

- What would you rather have after ten years of hard work: A large sum of money in the bank, or equity in a valuable business that would be relatively easy to sell?
- What's the least amount of money you could live on each month, provided that the mortgage, taxes, and utilities are paid for?

For most people who decide to run their own home-based publishing business, money is usually of secondary concern, at least in the beginning. Of course, it takes money to get a business up and running, regardless of your market, but most people who get into a home-based business are looking for a lifestyle change and satisfaction first and better income second. These priorities will help keep you motivated during the times when the money is slow in coming.

After the uncertainties of the first year of business, you can relax a little once the revenue is a bit more steady and you can predict your expenses, but you'll still find that it's necessary to reinvest much of your income back into the business in order to keep it growing. Unless you have a trust fund or a sizable side income, or hold onto your job or live off a spouse's or partner's income, you must learn to live frugally and get used to the idea of being cash-poor, at least for awhile.

Many people who would like to start their own home-based publishing businesses shy away from it for financial reasons; they're unwilling to risk part of their hard-earned savings or paychecks for a business that may or may not make any money for them. Even though you may be primarily motivated by the thought of being your own boss, running a business is all about financial risk—again, at least in the beginning. However, if you stick with an idea that is popular with a particular market, the possible payoff is great and financial success will come your way. If you want to have a good income, or even a great one, go ahead and start your own business. If you'd rather play it safe, then put your money in a CD or savings account. Even if you start your business with a thick stack of contracts and assurances of work from people who are already familiar with your abilities, I can tell you that there will still be days when things are going to be hairy. In the long run, however, if you're persistent and creative, you *will* be able to reach your financial goals as an entrepreneur.

Assessing Your Tolerance for Risk

Many people constantly fantasize about running their own home-based publishing business, but when it comes right down to it most will never take the necessary steps because they're reluctant to give up the security of a regular paycheck, health insurance, the familiarity with a particular lifestyle—you name it—even if they're unhappy with their current lives.

A person who falls into this category has a low tolerance for risk of any kind.

On the other hand, a person who can tolerate risk, and who even welcomes it to some degree, recognizes that even though he or she may do everything necessary to operate and promote the business successfully, there is still some element of risk that is beyond control, such as economic downturns and fickle weather. A risk taker accepts this as a normal part of doing business, and proceeds accordingly. What's your tolerance for risk? Find out by answering the following questions:

- Have you ever run a business of your own before? If so, how did you react when things slowed down? If you don't have experience in running a business, do you think you would react to a slowdown with panic or with the ability to constantly keep the big picture in mind?
- How would you react if you or a family member had to spend a week in the hospital and you didn't have health insurance because you needed the money to pay the mortgage?
- How important is it to you to have material items to validate your self-worth? What would you do if you were to suddenly lose them?

People who don't have a high tolerance for risky situations often see the world in black and white, with no room for gray areas. Certainly the prospect of quitting your job or cutting back to part-time so that you'll have the time to start your business is frightening, even to people who like some excitement. Lack of a safety net, the chances of success, and the chances of failure are probably only three of the concerns that are running through your head before you decide to start your business. However, if you're able to see these factors as challenges to overcome, and if you like to set your own schedule as well as not knowing what the next day or week will bring, you should be able to deal well with the unpredictable nature of being an entrepreneur.

The Skills You Will Need

As an entrepreneur involved in the publishing industry, the ability to communicate clearly and convincingly to potential customers is important to your success. If you know that you're lacking certain skills, it's important that you find someone who can fill those gaps. For example, if you prefer not to handle public relations, then hire someone to serve as your spokesperson. Though many entrepreneurs resist this from the outset, others embrace it so that they can concentrate on running and growing their business.

After years of experience running my own home-based publishing business, I can tell you that the most important skill you can have in this business is the ability to keep one eye focused on the seemingly endless details involved in keeping customers happy and generating new ideas, while keeping the other eye fixed on your long-term goals. This is not an easy thing to achieve, and indeed there are many times when I find myself veering off too far in one direction, like spending too much time thinking about how I'm going to add 100 more active buyers to my line of Litterature greeting cards in the next six months with nary a thought about the book I've committed to publish in the next season but is not near completion. If you're a born juggler, you'll probably find yourself in the same situation from time to time. Because you may not mind doing the grunt work so much (again, your home-based publishing business *is* your baby) and because stuffing envelopes and performing other menial tasks gives you a break from the hard work of pursuing new business and ensuring customer satisfaction, you may sometimes find yourself doing *too* much grunt work. And the opposite may happen, too, whenever you find that you're spending too much time trying to win over new accounts while your current clients feel a bit neglected.

Other skills that you'll need fall under the category of running a business, which I'll cover in detail in Part 3 (see page 83). You'll need to learn about cash flow, bookkeeping, and marketing, but again you can usually learn as you go, and also by asking other entrepreneurs from a variety of fields what business methods have worked best for them.

Even if you've never run a business before, you probably already know what you're good at from working for other people. And where your skills aren't as good, you'll be able to learn enough to get by. If you can afford to hire someone else to do work you're not good at, go ahead.

The Kind of Attitude You Will Need

In my opinion, the person best suited to be a home-based publishing entrepreneur is someone who's a cynical optimist, or, as some might say, an optimistic cynic. This is a person who has a positive attitude towards the world, but who also is not terribly surprised when things go wrong. When that happens, you spring into action and do whatever it takes to address the problem and get everything back to normal—until the next emergency, that is.

As a home-based publishing entrepreneur, you'll be dealing with a variety of people and situations as well as a business that is, in essence, operating twenty-four hours a day—at least in your mind. Surprises will come up from time to time, especially in the beginning. But as long as you maintain a positive attitude and remain alert to problems that need your immediate attention, while diplomatically putting off those that can wait, you'll be able to successfully keep your business running *and* maintain your equilibrium as well. And remember, at least once a week you should take a few hours to get away from the business, especially if you work from a home office; this goes a long way to help maintain a positive attitude.

What you'll need in terms of attitude to successfully run your home-based publishing business is a firm fixation on your field, a strong sense of who your customers are and what they need, and a strong belief in your subject. This kind of confidence will give you what it takes when you're dealing with current and potential customers, as well as those times when you need a heavy dose of motivation to pull you through the inevitable lulls in your business.

Your Assets and Liabilities

Before you start your home-based publishing business, it's a good idea to analyze your assets and liabilities—personal, financial, and those that involve your living space because you'll be working from home.

Starting up any business can be rough. If you want to find out how you're doing, you'll have to ask someone. Unsolicited feedback will usually come at some point from customers who are familiar with your business and what you provide. Even then, it will usually only come in a trickle. However, if you want real feedback early in your business endeavor, you will probably have to ask for it. Why not call some of your customers and potential customers and ask what they need, what they have no use for, and what it is that no one is currently providing?

Living in the same place where you work can also present a strain. Lots of people who run home-based businesses are frequently overwhelmed by their workload. One popular solution to such stress is to close the door to their office and take a break. Nevertheless, a home-based business will affect your entire family. How will you and your family cope with the adjustment? Good family communication and advance planning for private downtime together each day is a definite asset; it will help keep your goals about running a business in perspective.

As for money, experts say you should budget at least twice as much as you think you need. And by the way, the same advice also applies to the amount of time you'll need to get your business up and running. You'll need a financial cushion of at least several thousand dollars to cover both unexpected business and personal expenses, and financial experts usually recommend a much higher figure. There will always be expenses that you didn't budget for, and some emergencies will come up that require an immediate infusion of cash, like renting a booth at a trade show that had slipped your mind or taking advantage of a special deal on an ad in a trade publication. The important thing to know is that your liabilities can be addressed quickly if you have the assets—that is, the extra cash—to fix them as soon as possible.

How Your Lifestyle Will Change

Go back and reread the earlier section "A 'Typical' 8:00–5:00 Work Schedule." Life as you know it now will cease to exist once you start running your own business. One comment that I hear from home-based publishing entrepreneurs of all ages is that most tasks always take twice as long as they think they will, from training an employee to working on a new promotional story to waiting for direct mail responses to start rolling in. And if you're an impatient person to begin with—like me— these delays will occasionally make you crazy and unhappy with your business. And in the beginning, *everything* takes longer to get off the ground than you think, whether it's fine-tuning the content and design of your first ads or setting up your new phone system.

My advice is to be patient and work for the long run, because your lifestyle will eventually change for the better.

Most home-based entrepreneurs will start their businesses on a part-time basis while they're still holding down a full-time job. But if you've never worked at home or for yourself before, be prepared for a big surprise. The business will do its best to spill over into every corner of your life—that is, if you let it. That's why it's a good idea to take a break at least once a day and ignore the business at least one full day a week, even if your natural inclination is to work around the clock.

You may be gung ho about starting your own home-based publishing business, but you should take some time to consider how being an entrepreneur may affect your romantic relationships as well as your ties with friends and family, and how they might feel about your lack of time for them. You should be sure that your partner is in total agreement with your plans. While it's true that you may be doing most of the work of running your business, the fact is that you may need to ask them to pitch in every so often to help stuff envelopes and proofread copy, and generally tolerate your obsession with work. Make sure that they understand you're running the business for the benefit of the *entire* family. Even if one person in your household is opposed to the idea, you should work out your differences before you start your business. Play it safe: Before you proceed with your plans, be sure that you sit down with everybody that you're close to and get their feedback. Your family is also a good sounding board for future ideas you have for the business.

My Story

I work for myself because I've always been a bad employee.

I started working for myself when I was just eighteen. I was a magazine junkie, dropped out of New York University after only two months, and figured that writing freelance articles for magazines was a good way to earn a living.

I got spoiled early; I sold the first article I ever wrote and sent out. Even though it sold for only $25, that was all it took to give me the confidence to keep going and pursue larger markets.

Over the course of several years, I wrote many magazine articles for publications that you've probably never heard of, usually at $300 to $500 an article. I did this for awhile until I realized two things: first, I preferred marketing my article ideas to editors more than actually writing the articles; and second, I quickly figured out that while publishers had more expenses than I did, they also made more money and had more control. And so I decided to start publishing my own newsletter.

I stumbled into newsletter publishing before I even knew what I was doing. I first learned about newsletters when I was working part-time for a public relations firm in New York at the same time I was beginning to write articles for magazines. One of the company's accounts was a newsletter, and I would occasionally write press releases and make media phone calls on behalf of the newsletter in between helping out on the agency's other accounts, which included both doctors and financial planners. I spent the rest of my time away from the job trying to make it as a freelance magazine writer. All the books on writing that I had read always directed beginning writers to "write about what you know." At the time, what I knew about were the eating disorders anorexia nervosa and bulimia. Although I had written both personal experience stories and factual articles on these topics, I couldn't find any magazines that wanted to publish them; the articles I was selling at that point were short personal essays about city living and single life.

One afternoon, as I was sitting at my kitchen table looking at all of my rejected articles about eating disorders, the newsletter at work popped into my mind, and voilà, I decided to turn all of my rejected articles into a newsletter. Then I wrote press releases and sent them out to magazines and newspapers that might write about my newsletter.

These were the days before desktop computers, so I brought my articles to a typesetter and instructed him to assemble them in newsletter format. I also got stationery printed up, and within a week I was on my way.

Eating disorders were just beginning to be considered a newsworthy topic back then in 1982, so with my newsletter—which was titled *Consuming Passions*—I was among the first to ride the crest of mainstream media interest. Magazines as diverse as *Ms.*, *Woman's Day,* and *Seventeen* wrote small articles about my newsletter, always giving information about the cost of a subscription as well as my address. I was also interviewed on many radio and TV shows. But it wasn't until the singer Karen Carpenter died from the effects of anorexia nervosa in 1983 that I realized I was considered an expert on the subject. I was often the first person media people called for a quote. Indeed, many of the publishers I know tell me that they sometimes look over their shoulder when they are addressed as an expert in their field. I'll admit, becoming a publisher is the quickest way to become an expert in a certain field—that is, if you aren't one already.

I had started writing about eating disorders as a form of therapy and also as a way to launch my freelance writing career. As an editor of a regular publication, I was given magazine assignments by other editors—some of whom had rejected the articles I put into my first issue of *Consuming Passions*. I wrote not only about eating disorders, but also on other health topics, and eventually I turned to travel writing. After two years of publishing *Consuming Passions,* I began to tire of the subject. It had also ceased to be a personal problem for me. And so I sold the newsletter.

I spent the next few years writing for magazines, but the desire to be a publisher had remained in my blood. Between 1985 and 1995 I published and edited five more newsletters on subjects ranging from how to move from the city to the country (*Sticks*) to helping people who own small travel businesses, such as inns and B&Bs, market themselves better (*Travel Marketing Bulletin*).

In the early 1990s, I started writing books for other publishers; currently, I have twenty different titles in print with a number of different publishers, and I've written on everything from famous writers and their cats (*The Cat on My Shoulder*) to Vermont (*Vermont: Off the Beaten Path*) to Colin Powell (*In His Own Words: Colin Powell*). While I've enjoyed writing all these books, I still prefer to work as a publisher.

The first official (non-newsletter) product from my own company, Williams Hill Publishing, was produced in the fall of 1995: *The Business Traveler's Guide to Inns and B&Bs,* a Windows-based computer program that serves as a guide to more than 750 inns, B&Bs, and reservation services that cater to business travelers in the United States.

The one issue I've always had to face in running my own business is control: control over subject, content, marketing, and distribution. While I prefer to oversee all facets of publishing, from writing and editing to dealing with the printer to stuffing envelopes and taking them to the post office myself, I have begun to discover that with all of the different projects I want to tackle, it's necessary for me to farm out increasing amounts of work to independent contractors and relinquish some of my control.

Giving up some of my control became a real necessity in 1996, when I embarked on two entirely new areas of my home-based publishing business. The first was book publishing. Ever since I began writing books for other publishers, I realized that I wanted to actually publish books, written by myself and by other writers. There is more work involved, and certainly more financial risk, but ultimately there is more satisfaction and financial gain. The company I set up, Williams Hill Publishing, specializes in books about New England. With the help of outside designers and distributors, I published my first book in early 1997: *New Hampshire vs. Vermont.*

The second new area is a cat- and dog-related business called Litterature, in which I produce greeting cards for pets in three distinct categories: cards that pets can give to people, cards that people can give to pets, and cards that pets can give to pets. Given that I've written two cat books for other publishers and currently have six cats who keep me company as I work at home by myself, this seemed a natural development. I introduced my first line of 101 different cards in the fall of 1996. I also plan to publish books about cats and dogs under the Litterature imprint to sell to my existing wholesale customers and to consumers, as well as constantly pursue new markets. (See my Sample Business and Marketing Plans in the Appendix 1 for more information on how I launched this business.)

Many people tell me I do too much and that they think I get in over my head. Others believe I should just stick to one project. I work for myself because I don't have to answer to anybody, but also because I want to have fun. I'm free to pick projects that will be entertaining enough to pull me through the rough patches in the business. And I like to work by myself from my home office. My goal is not to run a humming factory with 300 employees; to me, that means I'd have to spend my time managing business growth and a large staff, not creating and thinking up new ideas.

My advice to you is to find something you love to do, create a niche within a particular field, and then twist it just enough so that you stand out from your competitors. If necessary, hire someone else to do the work you hate. And remember, every one of your business ideas is viable if *you* believe in it.

It's worked for me.

PART TWO

Your Publishing Choices

3

Booklets

Description of Business: A company that produces short-run booklets, usually containing fewer than seventy-two pages.

Ease of Startup: Easy. It's possible to write, print, and physically create the booklet at home on a demand basis as the orders come in.

Range of Initial Investment: If you already have a computer and desktop publishing system, you can get started for a few hundred dollars.

Time Commitment: Part-time.

Success Potential: Moderate. It's important to write compelling text for your booklets and also be able to give lots of concrete information, because that is what people expect from a booklet.

How to Market the Business: By targeting individuals and groups who would be interested in the topic of your booklet, selling at book and crafts fairs, and by promoting your booklets through the media.

The Pros: You're viewed as an expert on your topic.

The Cons: It's sometimes hard to get potential buyers to take you seriously because you have a booklet, and not a book.

Special Considerations: If you're kicking around an idea for a book, but don't want to invest the time and money that publishing a book requires, you can test your idea by first publishing a booklet as a teaser that shows what will be in the book.

The first thing that most people think of when they hear the word *publishing* is probably *books*. And I think that's a shame. The truth is, the cheapest and quickest way to get into publishing is by publishing booklets.

These small, helpful publications can be written and typeset on a standard desktop system and brought to your local copy shop to be bound with a simple cover. Even though you probably won't find them in a Barnes & Noble, most booklets offer specific information designed to help readers solve a particular problem, with such titles as *50 Recipes for Busy Working Moms, Easy Tips for Training Your New Puppy,* or *Simple Accounting for Small Businesses.* The writing in booklets needn't be fancy; in fact, it's discouraged. Booklets tend to have less than fifty pages to keep the design simple and the costs manageable, so there simply isn't space for superfluous writing. Instead, no-nonsense writing and lots of tips and advice are what work well in booklets.

Some people who are already running their businesses will frequently publish a booklet to hand out to their clients free of charge; these entrepreneurs consider booklets to be a way to promote their existing businesses. Management consultants and marketing experts are often asked to present their philosophies and policies for their clients; the easiest way to accomplish this is with a booklet.

Of course, if you have a good idea and lots of advice that can help people, you don't have to be a consultant to produce a booklet that sells and sells. No one knows this better than Paulette Ensign, who started her home-based publishing business, Organizing Solutions, with a simple idea, no money, and lots of determination. I'll let her tell her story herself:

"Way back in 1991, when my organizing business was already eight years old, I spotted an offer for a free copy of a booklet called *117 Ideas for Better Business Presentations.* Well, because I do business presentations and because the price was right, I sent for it. When it came, my first reaction was, 'I could knock something like this out about organizing tips.' Then I threw it in a drawer.

"Six months later I was sitting in my office, bored, baffled, and beaten down by the difficulty of selling my consulting services and workshops. I had no money. I mean *no* money! It was then that I remembered that little booklet. I had no idea how I was going to do it, but something hit me, and I knew I had to produce a booklet on organizing tips.

"I started dumping all the ideas I ever had about getting organized into a file on my computer. These were all pearls that came out of my mouth when I was with clients or when I did speaking engagements or seminars. I decided I could do one booklet on business organizing tips and another on household organizing tips—two sixteen-page tips booklets, each fitting into a #10 envelope. The first one was *110 Ideas for Organizing Your Business Life,* and the second one was *111 Ideas for Organizing Your Household.*

"My first print run was 250 copies and cost $300. That was the most expensive per-unit run I ever made, but I had to get samples to distribute to start making money. It took me a few months to pay the printer in full.

"I had no money to advertise. The only way I could think of selling the booklets was by sending a copy to magazines and newspapers, asking them to use excerpts and put an invitation at the bottom for readers to send $3 plus a self-addressed stamped envelope. Some publications actually followed through.

"Then the orders started dribbling in—envelopes with $3 checks in them or three $1 bills. This was great stuff. I remember the day the first one arrived. It was like manna from heaven: $3! Of course, the fact that it took about six months from first starting to write the booklets until the first $3 arrived somehow didn't matter at that moment.

"I cast seeds all over the place, hoping that some would sprout. I found directories of publications at the library and started building my list. Finally, in February of 1992, the big one hit. A twelve-page biweekly newsletter with 1.6 million readers ran nine lines of copy about my booklet. They didn't even use excerpts! That article sold 5,000 copies of my booklet. I distinctly remember the day I went to my P.O. box and found a little yellow slip. It said, "see clerk." A *tub* of envelopes had arrived that day, about 250 envelopes, as I recall—all with $3 in them.

"In April, that same biweekly newsletter ran a similar nine lines about my household booklet, and it started all over again. This time I sold 3,000 copies.

"'Round about June, I stopped and assessed what had happened. Was I making any money? By then, I had sold about 15,000 copies of the two organizing tips booklets, one copy at a time for $3. When I checked my financial records, I realized I had *not* generated a ton of money.

"And some of the lessons I had learned along the way were expensive ones. I didn't realize my bank was charging me twelve cents for each item deposited until I got my first bank statement with a service charge of $191.

"But some very wonderful things happened while selling those 15,000 copies. A public seminar company ordered a review copy to consider building another product from my booklet. As a result, I recorded an audio program based on my booklet. And I could sell that tape to my clients as well! In addition, it led to a twenty-minute interview on a major airline's in-flight audio program during November and December one year.

"As I was sorting through the envelopes I noticed a check for $1,000. It turns out a manufacturer's rep decided to send my booklets to his customers that year instead of an imprinted calendar.

"A company asked me to write a booklet that was more specific to their product line. I got speaking engagements from people who bought the booklet. I found out that the list of people who bought my booklet was a salable product.

"Things were starting to pick up. But let's go back to June, when I was taking stock of my situation. You know those advertising card decks in the mail? Well, I was so bored one day, I opened one. Glancing through it, I thought to myself, 'Gee, here's a company that ought to see my booklet. And here's another one, and another one.' I sent booklets to each.

"Less than a week later, a woman called. At first, it sounded like a prospecting call. Fortunately, I wasn't too abrupt with her. She was calling to ask me for the cost of producing 5,000 customized copies of my booklet for an upcoming trade show. She wanted to know if I could match a certain price.

"I slightly underbid her price, so she was thrilled, and we agreed to the deal. I thought, 'Ooh, this will be easy to sell large quantities now.' Wrong. It was another three to four months until the next large-quantity sale. The organization hosting the trade show had previously rejected my booklet because I wasn't in their industry. Now my buyer had bought 5,000 copies of my booklet, with my company information in it, to distribute at that trade show. I loved it!

"One day, a guy I know from a major consumer mail-order catalog company said, 'Why don't you license us reprint rights to your booklet. We can print it cheaper than you, so if you charged us a few cents a unit, you wouldn't have to do production.' Well, eighteen months later, after lots of zigging and zagging, that sale happened: a nonexclusive agreement for them to print 250,000 copies. We exchanged a ten-page contract for a five-digit check. They provided the booklet free with any purchase in one issue of their catalog and had a 13 percent increase in sales for that issue. They were happy. I was happy. I looked for other licensing prospects (even though it took eighteen months for this sale to happen, and the five-digit check was in the low five digits, not enough to sustain me).

"Around spring of 1993, I designed a class on how to write and market booklets, and wrote an eighty-page manual. The class was small and mostly made up of people I knew. They paid me a fee, and I had a chance to test-run the class. So now I had another new product: an eighty-page manual, a blueprint of how I had sold more than 50,000 copies of my booklet without spending a penny on advertising.

"I like teaching, so now I had a new topic besides the organizing seminar I had been presenting. I also like traveling. I took the three-hour class on the road and had great fun doing it. I toured the country for about two years, teaching six to eight classes a year. I found many people who had written interesting booklets on all kinds of topics. Some have hired me to write a customized marketing plan for their booklets or to coach them by phone to develop their booklet businesses.

"Midway through that year (August 1994), I discovered CompuServe. My sole purpose for getting online was to market my business. The third day I was online, I saw a forum message from a guy in Italy who had a marketing company there. He told me his client base was small businesses and companies who served small businesses. I told him I had a booklet he might find useful. I sent it to him, he liked it, and we struck a deal. He translated, produced, and marketed it, and then paid me royalties on all sales. In January 1997 he wired several thousand dollars to my checking account. He made the first sale of 105,000 copies to a magazine that bundled a copy of my booklet with one issue of their publication.

"That meant I had sold more than 400,000 copies of my booklet, in two languages, without spending a penny on advertising.

"One slow week, I posted a message on some CompuServe forums about the story of the Italian booklet as an example of an online success story. Even though blatant selling is not allowed on forums, creating mutually beneficial relationships is. I had received money from someone I had never spoken to and had only communicated with online, by fax, by earth mail, and through electronic funds transfer, so that made it relevant for discussion.

"Some folks who read those postings replied that they would be interested in doing the same thing with my booklet, but in French and in Japanese. This had never even dawned on me. I now have discussions open with people in ten different countries; within 3.5 years, this has grown into a $250,000 business. Once these relationships are established, it makes sense to discuss brokering some other booklets, like those written by people in my classes or by people I've coached, or by those who have bought my publishing manual.

"I've also discovered other opportunities for my booklet content in other formats.

- Two different companies who produce laminated guides (one hinged, the other spiral bound) licensed my content and will launch these in 1998. (They are also interested in other content, so I expect to broker the content of other booklet writers.)
- An in-flight video information service is interested in expanding their content and is looking at my proposal.
- I've created a new division in my company called Tips Products International.
- I've started writing tips for booklet production and other uses by developing three different packages of 25 to 100 tips with recommended uses. These tips packages are created from the clients' materials recycled into tips or by doing original research for them.
- I write customized marketing plans for other people's booklets.

"At the beginning of this business, I never could have written a business plan for how this has all unfolded. It arose naturally out of the continuing promotion I did for the booklets."

4

Books

Description of Business: A company that publishes a small number of books—sometimes fewer than one each year—usually on related subjects, which becomes a niche within a niche.

Ease of Startup: Difficult. You need equipment to process words and typeset, a trustworthy printing company, a talented cover and page designer, a good topic, and lively writing.

Range of Initial Investment: $10,000 for your first title; usually less for subsequent titles.

Time Commitment: Part-time to write and produce the books; full-time to market.

Success Potential: Moderate. The more people you know, and the more outgoing you are, the better your chances for success. If you can be persuasive in a lot of different situations, you can do quite well.

How to Market the Business: Through publicity, bookstores, specialty shops, even at flea markets, or with groups that have a special interest in the subjects of your books. A growing market is to sell books in bulk to companies that will use them as premiums to enhance their own image.

The Pros: There's a book in everyone; publishing it yourself will ensure it gets out.

The Cons: It's expensive to publish a book. Plus, with the tens of thousands of new books published each year, you have to be loud and/or different in order to be heard.

Special Considerations: Contrary to what you may think, bookstores may constitute a very small percentage of your sales.

"Everyone has a book inside of them."
"Don't judge a book by its cover."

These and countless other clichés that cite books are proof positive that our society is still in thrall with the published book. In 1996, an estimated 60,000 books were published for all types of people and on all subjects imaginable. Put in more concrete terms, for every single day of that year, 165 new books were introduced to the market, all looking for readers. Combined with another frequently cited statistic that more than half of Americans don't buy even one book over the course of the year, some publishing entrepreneurs might read these figures and become disheartened. However, the news is actually quite good for new book publishers. The big New York publishers still concentrate on finding and publishing the next Stephen King or the next guide to catching a man (after the runaway success of the book *The Rules*), and on these grounds, small publishers simply do not have the resources to compete effectively.

But the niche markets are left wide open to the small publishers, who target markets that would seem microscopic to the big guys. Say you have an idea for a book on how to start a floral business because, after all, that's how you've spent the last fifteen years of your life. Great. You're an expert. If you sell a couple thousand copies a year, you'll be a success. To a publisher the size of Random House or Simon & Schuster, however, 2,000 copies is nothing but a failure.

In fact, many small book publishers that specialize in niche markets today know that their books are unlikely to ever see the inside of a bookstore. Marketing directly to your likely customers through publicity, direct mail, and other means, will not only net you more money than through bookstore distribution, but you also have the advantage of building a list of your customers, which will be quite valuable if you choose to expand your publishing empire; after all, if they bought a book on the floral business, they might also buy an audiotape, subscribe to a newsletter, and attend a seminar on the same subject.

Profile

Jim Hoskins
Maximum Press
Gulf Breeze, Florida

One of the fastest growing topics for publishers of any type concerns computers: how to use them, how to program them, and even how to use them to market your business. Jim Hoskins started his company Maximum Press with this in mind.

Hoskins has been involved in the computer and high-tech fields from its earliest days. He worked at IBM for ten years and had a degree in electrical engineering. While still at IBM, Hoskins wrote a book about a product he was developing, and the book was eventually published by John Wiley & Sons, a large business publisher in New York. He wrote a few other books about IBM products while still an employee, and he transferred within the company to Gulf Breeze, Florida, where he took a marketing job. This is where he began to contemplate his future.

"I was trying to figure out what to do, because at that point, I was on the management fast track to become an executive at IBM," he said. "So I took a poll and asked other executives if they would follow the same path if they had it to do over again. They all said no because they moved a lot, worked too much, and never saw their families."

Hoskins took a look at the books he wrote and saw them as alternatives to the gerbil-wheel lifestyle at IBM. He then took a one-year leave of absence from the company to write full time and start his own publishing company specializing in computer books. Six months into his leave of absence, IBM offered an incentive plan to employees to quit during one of its early downsizing waves. Hoskins accepted the offer and never returned to the company. That was in 1992. In January of 1993, he incorporated as Maximum Press and started his publishing company at full speed with IBM as his first client. He could have concentrated on writing books, but he saw that you could make more money on the publishing side than on the writing side.

That first year, at the age of thirty-four, Hoskins published three books. The first book he published was about a software package that IBM had produced for the manufacturing world. "I made IBM commit up front to the number of books they would buy, and I made sure that their commitment alone was enough to make the book profitable," says Hoskins. For awhile, he thought he would only publish books that relied on these deals with IBM so that he could build up some cash to publish the books he really wanted to do. And since the books were only of interest to IBM, Hoskins couldn't begin to think about bookstore distribution.

But once he had enough cash to publish books for consumers, which obviously provided him with a larger audience than just IBM, he began to plan these books and pursue bookstore distribution. In 1994, he signed up with Publishers Group West, a major distributor for small publishers, which gave him access to a whole new market that he didn't have before. He was able to broaden the subjects of his company's titles just based on the distribution. His first consumer-oriented title, *Marketing on the Internet*, has sold 12,000 copies in a year. Future books will include an Internet shopping guide and other consumer-oriented titles that will sell well through bookstore distribution as well as in other markets.

In 1996, Hoskins had plans to publish from eight to ten new books in two distinct markets: one directed at IBM and trade, and the other directed away from IBM completely. Since he began his company, Hoskins has worked out of his home office, though it hasn't always been easy. He converted a spare bedroom into an office. From the beginning, he has always had at least one employee to "take care of the things that I didn't want to do myself," which included bookkeeping. He had the room remodeled to look like a regular office and bought office furniture and a professional phone system. It worked for awhile, but in time, Hoskins started to dislike having an employee traipse in and out of his house during the day. So he solved the problem by building a 750-square-foot office suite onto his home with enough room to accommodate up to three employees. More importantly, this office has its own separate entrance so he feels his work life doesn't interfere with his personal life.

As it turned out, Hoskins's first employee was embezzling from the business by forging checks, so he fired him and got the money back. "It was troubling to have someone you're trying to nurture take advantage of you like that," he says, and has learned to be more careful when hiring employees.

Hoskins serves as the publisher and editor at Maximum Press, and has other people to handle finance and administration, management, customer service, and marketing and publicity. He farms out the production work on his books to a local subcontractor, and intends to grow the company by using subcontractors or employees where appropriate.

"I tried subcontracting the company's marketing efforts, but that didn't work because the database for this branch needed to be available to everyone in the office," he said. "I also wanted to be able to oversee the development of the marketing database so it could be done correctly. But even if we become as big as Microsoft, I still intend to work out of my home office and have satellite offices for the overflow."

Hoskins hasn't noticed that his youth has affected his ability to run his business or the willingness of others to work with him. "Being younger and weaned on computers, I might be more willing to exploit technology than someone who's fifty and just starting a business," he said. "But then again, I have a friend who told me his grandmother refused to talk on the phone because she didn't like to talk into a box. Change comes hard to some people. Younger entrepreneurs have an advantage that way."

What surprises Hoskins the most about being an entrepreneur is the sheer volume of opportunities out there every day that he has to choose from. "Knowing that my choices are going to make the difference between life and death, I want to do them all, but I don't want to spend my life doing them all," he says. "I *could* do more than I am right now, but I don't want to work eighty hours a week.

"*Nothing* is more valuable than your time," he continues. "If you make a lot of money and have a successful business but have no time left over, you lose. The ideal mix is to have a business selling products and information, but not time, because time is more valuable than money. I can launch products and they'll live their own little lives while I'm not working. But if I'm a dentist, if I'm not working, I'm not making money."

Hoskins believes that by running an information business from his home, he has a degree of flexibility that others only dream of. "If I take a day off, I know it's not directly affecting my income," he says. He also has a seven-year-old son and triplets who are still in diapers. In addition to running the business and watching his kids, Hoskins also goes for an hour bike ride each day. However, he considers it to be part of his work day because he brings a tape recorder with him and says he thinks of many ideas during that hour.

"Coming from the corporate world, I know how hard corporate jobs can be on families," he says, "and I don't think that it's healthy or good in the long term for either the country or for society. I don't think that businesses will be able to continue long term in that vein. The people who work for me are mothers, and whenever their children are sick, there's never any question of whether they have to come in to work that day. If there's a class party, they can leave in the middle of the day. Their children come here after school and do homework, and play with my children sometimes. There are a lot of people who are not in the workforce who can't justify wrecking their families for the sake of a job. I'm happy that I'm able to give them an option by working here, and they just love it. I don't pay huge salaries, but because I have a family orientation I'm going to be able to get good employees at bargain prices. After all, I'm helping to support their families."

His advice to other people who want to start a home-based publishing business is to go slowly and save as much money as you can before you start. He recommends that you use that time to plan and think. "Pick a publishing niche business that positions your lifestyle the way you want it to be," he advises.

5

Greeting Cards

Description of Business: A company that produces greeting cards and other stationery products, such as notepaper, wrapping paper, and ribbon.

Ease of Startup: Moderate. If you start on a small-scale basis, you'll have less money tied up in inventory, but it will take longer to get established since many retailers and others in the distribution channel won't take you seriously if you carry fewer than eighty different cards.

Range of Initial Investment: To start with a line of twenty different cards, $5,000. To start with one hundred different cards, promotional catalogs, rack display cards, and other retailer tools, $25,000 and up.

Time Commitment: Full-time, especially if you choose to sell direct to consumers and to the wholesale market.

Success Potential: Moderate. If you have your eye on widespread wholesale distribution, be aware that it may take years to build up to that point. In the meantime, developing a following with your own customers can convince distributors and retailers to stock your cards. As always, focusing on a particular market will help.

How to Market the Business: By servicing your sales reps promptly and attentively, providing attractive deals to retailers, exhibiting at trade shows for the gift trade, and producing catalogs that advertise an ever-changing line of new cards and other stationery products.

The Pros: It's a fun business, and you're helping people to express their feelings to another person (or, in my case, to a cat or dog).

The Cons: It's a lot harder than it looks. Plus, greeting cards are very fragile objects, and can get mangled and damaged during shipping and while on display in a rack. Retail accounts require the option of returning unsold seasonal cards after a holiday is over.

Special Considerations: Study the market and try to make your cards different from everything else that's out there.

The greeting card business is a fun business, but also a highly competitive one. And it can be extremely lucrative if you hit the industry just right.

Here are the facts about the industry, as provided by the Greeting Card Association, based in Washington, D.C.

- Approximately 7.4 billion greeting cards are purchased annually by American consumers, generating roughly $6.3 billion in U.S. retail sales.
- Of the total greeting cards purchased annually, roughly half are seasonal and the remaining half are everyday cards. Sales of everyday cards, especially non-occasion cards, are on the increase.
- The most popular card-sending holidays are, in order, Christmas, Valentine's Day, Easter, Mother's Day, and Father's Day.
- People of all ages and types exchange greeting cards. Women purchase approximately 85 percent of all greeting cards, and the average card purchaser is a woman in her middle years, although this demographic picture may be changing.

- Cards range in price from 35¢ to $10.00, with the average card retailing for around $1.50. Cards featuring special techniques and new technologies are at the top of this price scale.
- The average person receives thirty cards per year, eight of which are birthday cards.
- Estimates indicate that there are around 1,500 greeting card publishers in America, ranging from major corporations to small family organizations. Greeting Card Association members together account for approximately 90 percent of the industry market share.

The greeting card industry is as varied as the thousands of individuals who are pursuing the field. Many people who enter the field are artists who desire to circulate their paintings, drawings, and photographs beyond their own studios. It's inexpensive to put together a portfolio of ten to twenty different greeting cards, and so many people have traveled down this road.

However, because it's so easy to get started in the greeting card business—and much more difficult to maintain business and grow beyond the common initial venues of local stores and crafts fairs—retailers who are in charge of making purchasing decisions see an awful lot of unprofessionally produced cards out in the market, which may explain the lukewarm reception that many novice greeting card producers get when they first burst onto the market.

Admittedly, as I write this, I'm only in my first year of running a greeting card business, and that in an extremely small niche. However, I have learned much about what to focus on and what to avoid in the course of selling my greeting cards. So here goes.

Profile

Lisa Shaw
Litterature
Grafton, New Hampshire

As is the case with every other kind of publishing business I've run in the course of fifteen years, I've never been a good one for taking my own advice. I always come up with the idea first, do a little research, and then plunge right in. This is what happened when I decided to start a greeting card company.

Being a slave to a number of cats—currently six—and having authored two books about cats for other book publishers, I had always had my eye out for a publishing business I could start that somehow involved cats, and dogs as well. It wasn't until the holiday season of 1994 when lightning struck.

My husband Dan and I were playing with the two cats we had at the time, Margo and Squggy, when suddenly Dan said he thought it was a shame that the cats hadn't received any Christmas cards. We started to think about all of the different occasions when it would be nice to send a greeting card to a cat or dog—or to receive one from them. We filled several sheets of paper with ideas and then decided to start a company making cards for pets— they could send these cards to you and to each other, or you could use them to convey news about your pets to your friends.

My next decision was what to use as art for the front of the cards. I had worked with a cartoonist on a previous humor book about pigs and I thought his style would work well. I told him of my idea, he sent a few rough sketches, but then I decided I shouldn't use him: What if he decided to bail out after the first line of cards? I wanted a consistent look to the cards, and didn't want to have to rely on one artist.

At the time, I was dealing in antiques and collecting antique postcards of my town. One day, I was leafing through the Grafton postcards at a local antique mall when I noticed a file card a few rows over for cat postcards. I liked what I saw and spent the next three months buying up postcards with cats, and later for dogs, after several friends told me of many occasions when they had altered a human card to give to their dogs. The big advantage to using these original postcards is that they were essentially copyright-free: they were produced in the 1890s and early 1900s, and the companies that owned them went out of business around the time of World War I. So I didn't have to pay anyone to use these illustrations, and the pictures were absolutely charming and very different from any other greeting cards that I had seen on the market.

My next step was to come up with the various categories of cards. I went to a few of the cat- and dog-specific Internet mailing lists and groups and asked people to tell me about the different occasions when they had sent a card to a cat or dog. I came up with fourteen categories for each, including adoption announcements, holiday cards, "get well soon" cards, cards to say thanks to the vet and groomer, as well as sympathy cards.

I had originally thought to produce only forty different cards in my first line. However, once I included dogs, I decided to go for broke (literally!) and produce 100 different cards.

One long day, I took my 900 postcards and started to match them up with specific categories: for instance, one postcard worked better as a humorous card, while another was great for a vet appointment reminder card. Then I had to be somewhat equitable: If I had a happy birthday card for a cat, I also had to have one for a dog. And then there were occasions I had thought of, but had no card to match. And so I went back out into the trenches of the antique malls and postcard shows.

Later I found a graphic designer who scanned the postcards into his desktop publishing program, cleaned up the imperfections, and laid them out for the printer, which would include some verse on the inside of the card and the identifying information—including a UPC (Universal Product Code, or bar code)—on the back. Most retailers and all of the chains require UPCs on every product they sell. He also helped to design the twenty-eight-page catalog I would use to solicit both consumers and retailers.

Once we were done with the cards and catalogs, it was time to design the display cards for the racks that would tell the buyer if a card was a dog adoption card or a cat sympathy card. Plus, I decided to produce both horizontal and vertical cards, so this meant that we needed at least fifty-six different types of rack cards: fourteen different categories, one horizontal, one vertical, for both cats and dogs.

The display cards that are placed in a holder above the rack—called *toppers* in the trade—were simple in contrast, but they were yet another thing to consider. They contained our company name, a brief description, and our logo.

Once everything was at the printer, it was time to find some suppliers, such as the company that would supply me with greeting card racks. I later learned that most wholesale orders tend to be for individual cards in quantities of one dozen each, and not for rack plans, since many retailers either already own the racks or will place the cards in a long floor rack model, not the spinning display racks that I think display the cards at their best.

I designed the wholesale order form for Litterature with a simple spreadsheet program, allowing one line for each different card; each line contains the unit number that I've assigned it plus a brief description of the card.

I also decided to go for broke at the time and develop a few gift packages that my customers might be interested in. I had heard about people throwing birthday parties for their cats and dogs, and so I designed a party kit that contained party invitations (our own, of course!), some toys and treats, and party favors for guests to bring home to their own pets. Also included was a mug with our logo on it along with some catnip or dog biscuits, which means that whenever an order comes in, we always ask, "Is that for a cat or a dog?"

One additional design we used for the cards included paw prints on both sides of the envelope, along with a very tiny version of our logo and the Litterature name. We had to follow certain postal regulations, but I thought it added a nice touch.

The fateful day came when the cards were ready to be picked up from the printer. Since I knew I was going to market the cards to consumers, I had drawn up a press kit (see Chapter 16 for details) and developed a mailing list of about 500 media people.

My first press mailing resulted in some media attention and lots of requests for free catalogs. I brought those newspaper articles—from the *San Francisco Chronicle, Boston Globe*, and the *Wall Street Journal*—with me to a couple of pet industry trade shows where I exhibited the cards. I made some contacts with wholesale accounts, sold some cards, and met some sales reps who were interested in selling the cards. I also met a magazine editor who later wrote a story about the cards, which resulted in some business.

The next step was to pursue wholesale accounts more aggressively. Armed with the positive media reviews, I bought a directory of sales reps who sold to the gift trade, and sent each a catalog, sample card, order form, and press clips. From this first round, I signed up fifty sales reps located all over the country.

As I write this account, roughly six months after I began the business, I can say that I've learned a lot about the greeting card business and know that I still have a lot more to learn. It's a lot like other forms of publishing, but it's also different because I couldn't simply sell the cards to consumers. I had to sell to wholesale accounts, and selling to retailers is an entirely different game than selling directly to consumers.

Greeting cards are also different because I create the products once and then continue to market them, which is unlike the newsletters I published and edited, which required me to continually introduce a new product—in this case, a new issue—every couple of months while continuing to market it.

One caveat about marketing greeting cards as I have: Response from consumers has been pretty low because people just aren't accustomed to ordering individual greeting cards out of a catalog. Usually, they go into a gift shop, select a gift, and then wander over to the greeting card department. It's frequently difficult to teach people a new way of doing things, even if it's more convenient for them.

So, as any good home-based publishing entrepreneur should do, I've decided to branch out. In addition to the cards, I've sold a number of birthday party kits, personalized Christmas stockings, and writing kits for cats and dogs (a rubber stamp paw print, an ink pad, and a selection of greeting cards). I'm going to continue to introduce new gift items for pets: The latest are gift baskets to celebrate a special day in your dog or cat's life, a dog bath basket, and sympathy baskets to be sent to a person who's just lost a cat or dog.

I'll continue to market to both consumers and wholesale markets. Whenever Litterature is written up in a consumer publication, I'll inevitably receive calls from bookstores, pet stores, and gift shops that are interested in carrying the cards.

As with all of the home-based publishing businesses I've run, I've mostly learned as I've gone along. As some ideas and marketing methods don't pan out, I scrap them and look for more.

One thing I have learned is never to say no. You never know who's watching, and whether a small sale to a consumer will lead to a huge order from a chain store. That's what keeps me going, along with the fact that I never stop learning about the business.

6

Magazines

Description of Business: A company that publishes a magazine on a specific topic that appears anywhere from biweekly to quarterly.

Ease of Startup: Moderate. If you have a desktop computer system, you can write, lay out, and print an issue in a short period of time. Distribution—free or paid—frequently requires outside help.

Range of Initial Investment: $3,000 and up.

Time Commitment: Full-time. Many publishers focus on editorial and production, hiring an outside sales staff for advertising.

Success Potential: Difficult. Many magazines are unable to draw the amount of advertising and/or subscribers necessary to cover costs.

How to Market the Business: With sufficient distribution, trades with radio stations, promotional and event tie-ins with other businesses, and a quality publication.

The Pros: You're viewed as a voice of the community.

The Cons: It's hard work. Collecting money from advertisers.

Special Considerations: In the last decade, magazines have become more narrow. Find a topic and an audience that's not being addressed.

Ah, the wonderful world of magazines. In the old days, *Saturday Review* and *Reader's Digest* reigned. Today, it's *Snowshoe Quarterly*, *My Ferret*, and *Dental Hygienist Leisure Time*, which shows you how far people have taken the idea of niche publishing.

Publishing what we all regard as a magazine—four-color, glossy, with lots of ads—is perhaps the most difficult and time-consuming type of publishing. It's almost impossible to run it as a one-person business, because advertising, newsstand distribution, editorial, design, and circulation are so labor-intensive in and of themselves, not to mention the work handling the financial end of things. This is true even for very small magazines. A woman I know who published a beautiful four-color magazine to publicize the town of Woodstock, Vermont, had a veritable force of warm bodies helping her meet quarterly deadlines.

Four out of every five new magazines introduced each year will fail by their second birthday. Don't be afraid to start small, but be sure to create a demand from your readers, which will, in turn, create a demand from advertisers who want to reach them. If you haven't already penned a few freelance articles for some small or regional magazines, then get moving. Writing an article for a particular publication will give you an idea how to slant a story towards a particular type of reader, which you can then extrapolate into creating an entire magazine. By the way, a great beginning exercise for your proposed magazine is to describe your reader in twenty-five words, and then draw up a sample table of contents for your first six issues.

Profile

Choices Magazine
Gloria Bursey
Grand Rapids, Michigan

When Gloria Bursey decided to stop publishing a regional women's magazine called *Glory*, she told herself she never wanted to publish another magazine as long as she lived. Then she became a widow and had no choice but to start looking for work. "I was known as a writer in this area, but no one wanted to hire me," she remembers. "It seems they would rather hire somebody younger, to whom they didn't have to pay as much money."

At the same time she looked around for advice about retirement and aging issues, but didn't have much luck. "What I saw out there didn't tell me very much," she recalls, "and people are living longer and have much more retirement time than before." She thought about breaking her promise and starting another magazine, this time on retirement and aging.

Bursey began by talking with seniors around town to find out what they would like to see in a magazine geared toward them. She also met with prospective advertisers. She wrote up some columns and features, and designed the layout on a Macintosh computer (when she published *Glory* she had to rely on typesetters). Before she knew it, she was publishing another magazine.

Choices is a sixteen-page monthly newsmagazine printed on paper that's of higher quality than newsprint. She prints about 23,000 copies each month and has a circulation of about 40,000, due to people lending their copies to others. Most of her sales staff of five are retired, and she pays them a 23 percent commission.

Though Bursey still writes the editorial and an occasional article, she relies mainly on outside writers to fill the pages. She's never had a problem finding reliable writers, because people will write or call to suggest stories. "*Choices* has a mix of columns and features," explains Bursey. "We recently featured Ms. Senior Michigan, who's in her seventies." The magazine also includes a financial column, a travel story, a health column, and stories geared toward singles. Though she is starting to include some controversial stories in the magazine—about hospices and Medicaid—she tries to keep the tone upbeat. "I think too many papers are negative," she points out.

There's also a calendar of local events and a column by a local man who's ninety-three. She pays her writers $25 for a column, $35 for a short article, and up to $125 for a long story. Each issue is free. Bursey distributes the magazine in over 200 places within a sixty-mile radius, including grocery stores, department stores, restaurants, and senior centers. Even though it's a free publication, she still strives to make the cover inviting. It started out in black-and-white and is now four-color.

"I started the magazine because I'm a writer," she says, but admits she was a little bit ahead of herself because businesses weren't used to gearing their advertising toward people over fifty. Now they're used to the idea. The magazine has a fifty-fifty advertising to editorial ratio: Each page contains half ads and half editorial. In general, the smaller the publication is, the more you have to load it with advertising. "As it gets larger," Bursey points out, "you make more money and you can have more editorial."

Advertisers are billed when the issue comes out. Some take a while to pay, however, and she turns some over to an attorney for collection. "Our policy is if they don't pay by the second ad, they can't place another ad until they've paid. If it's a new business, I suggest we get payment in advance."

Bursey also writes a column for a local newspaper, which she is trying to syndicate to more mainstream papers in the region. She also does some photography for the magazine, working out of her home. She's looking into the possibility of expanding *Choices* to cover the entire state of Michigan, but then she'd have to approach a completely different type of advertiser to make it fly. "I love publishing because it keeps me active in the community," reports Bursey. "I'm in the center of everything because *I'm* the media."

She thinks magazine publishing would be a great business for a couple to run, with one keeping the books and the other selling ads. "Even if you aren't a writer, you can always find people to write for you. After all it's impossible to do everything. People are aging more slowly these days—I call it *Star*

Trek time, or time that we didn't think we'd have. Occasionally I meet editors who do everything on a magazine, and I don't know how they do it."

7

Newsletters

Description of Business: A company that publishes one or more subscription newsletters that focus on a very specific field.

Ease of Startup: Moderate. You need one sample issue to start.

Range of Initial Investment: $500 if you already have a computer.

Time Commitment: Part- or full-time

Success Potential: Easy. Be sure you fill a niche that nobody else is addressing and have the marketing plan to back it up.

How to Market the Business: Through direct mail, publicity, conferences, lectures, and advertising.

The Pros: It's satisfying to have people pay for what you have to say.

The Cons: Sometimes it's difficult to get subscribers to renew.

Special Considerations: Newsletter publishing is for people who have a particular interest and are able to address it in very specific ways.

Publishing a newsletter will appeal to anyone who believes passionately enough in a particular topic to want to invest their time and money in it. It's also important that you enjoy letting other people know how you feel about your subject. Sometimes, in fact, your interest may be close to an obsession. Unlike other publications, it's possible to be as opinionated as you want in your newsletter, and your readers will love you for it.

Even though publishing a newsletter involves a lot of hard work, the rewards are ample: instant expert status, in-depth knowledge on a particular topic, and what is effectively your own forum in each and every issue. I'll warn you now that the skills you'll develop by publishing your own newsletter, and the headiness of having your own publication, will get into your blood.

The good news is that it's both cheap—if you want it to be— and easy to start publishing a newsletter on a certain topic to sell on a subscription basis. However, after you begin, you may frequently encounter one or all of the following reactions:

- Is that all there is?
- Do you really expect me to pay that much money for a subscription?
- Why don't you just publish a magazine instead of pretending that you want to be one?

Then there's the flip side of the newsletter business. Because, by its very merits, a newsletter is supposed to deliver concise information about a very narrow subject, those people who are interested in that subject frequently react with manic enthusiasm:

- They tear open the envelope the minute they retrieve it from the mailbox, sit down on the floor, and read it right then and there, cover to cover.
- They hoard every copy and keep them in fireproof boxes.
- They write to the publisher and ask what they need to do to become a lifetime subscriber.

Today it's estimated that anywhere from 100,000 to 200,000 different newsletters are published each year. Even I was shocked when I read these figures, but when you start to think about the wide variety of newsletters that you probably already receive—from the PTA, your church, your dentist, or another that contains nothing but chocolate recipes, as well as the one your company publishes for its employees and stockholders four times a year—well, then, this figure begins to make sense.

Typically, a newsletter is published about a specific subject or for a particular group. As such, it may go into great detail on the subject, details that may bore the casual observer but will thrill a person who's seriously interested in the topic. A newsletter can be as brief as one page or as long as thirty-two—and I've seen newsletters that are even longer. A newsletter may be published once a year or once a day, may be created with a typewriter or the latest in desktop publishing software, and may be run off with an old-fashioned mimeograph machine or on fancy textured paper with several colors of ink or even color photos. And it could have 20 readers or 200,000 readers.

A newsletter can also be a perfect way to impart information to members of an association who rely on it for news about the group and upcoming events. However, this is a different type of newsletter, one that's not sold by subscription. A business may also decide to create a promotional newsletter to inform current customers about new products, or to attract new customers. Church groups and trade organizations often use newsletters to keep their members informed about news that concerns the group. Some newsletter publishers actually get started by offering to produce newsletters for these types of organizations, which is a great way to generate some revenue and develop your publishing skills. However, since it is usually the burning desire to get your voice and opinions—and advice—out there to readers, most of the information here pertains to publishing and editing a newsletter to sell by subscription.

Some people may think that you want to publish a newsletter because you can't afford or are too lazy to publish a magazine, but the truth is that the subjects of most newsletters are far too specific to warrant the expense and size of a typical magazine, which is supported more by its advertising revenue than by subscription fees. In addition, the majority of newsletters don't accept advertising.

But a newsletter offers several advantages over a magazine, which is why there are at least ten times more newsletters than magazines. Here are just a few advantages:

- Since you're not supported by advertising, you don't have to worry about offending one of them by something you may say in the newsletter.
- Since newsletter production is pretty straightforward, the amount of time you'll spend on writing, designing, and printing it is much less than a magazine. Given this flexibility, you can add late-breaking news up to an hour before delivery to the printer or copy shop.
- The more specific you get in your newsletter articles, the more your readers will love it, which means you'll get to explore all the topics too insignificant for a larger audience. For instance, in a newsletter about model trains, an article about one of the early designers would be welcomed. In a more general magazine about hobbies, it would probably be too specific.

While subscription rates will be your main source of income, ancillary products such as special reports, seminars, books, and tapes can reap great profits. You can produce them yourself or buy them at wholesale rates from other publishers—and the more you sell lowers your cost per unit. Special reports of four to ten pages can range about a dollar a page, audiotapes of special programs can be priced from $10 to $25, and the profit margin if you sell books by other publishers can be as high as 40 percent, as long as you charge extra for shipping and handling.

Though seminars can be a lot of work, they bring in extra income from current subscribers and attract potential customers who may buy some of your products and also subscribe to your newsletter. A seminar can be anything from a ninety-minute evening program held in a rented room at the local YMCA to a full-fledged weeklong convention, complete with a full roster of experts in your field who give workshops, a trade show with hundreds of exhibitors, and other special social programs for attendees.

Some seminar organizers charge an admission fee—especially when the seminar lasts a day or more—while others let people in for free in the hopes that they'll subscribe to their newsletter or sign up for a later seminar that *does* charge a fee. The custom is to offer a discount if an attendee signs up well in advance of the workshop, and to charge full price up to a week before the seminar begins and for admission at the door. In any case, the seminar producer doesn't expect to profit off the admission fees, but instead hopes to raise enough money to cover the cost of the room rental as well as the money spent to promote the event.

When setting prices on the products you sell, remember to be flexible, especially if expected profits don't immediately materialize. Keep in mind that in some cases—particularly newsletters for businesspeople and investors—if you set the price too low, potential readers may be turned off because they may perceive it to have no value.

Profile

Elaine Floyd
Newsletter News & Resources
St. Louis, Missouri

Elaine Floyd was one of the pioneers in the newsletter business back in the early 1980s. She wrote and edited nonsubscription newsletters to use as a sales tool. She produced her newsletters on the first Macintosh computer using the first version of Pagemaker, a common desktop publishing program.

Floyd's background was in engineering, and she worked in sales and marketing for a high-tech company in Nashville. "I was driving all over the south, and I was so busy that I frequently forgot to tell my clients everything they needed to know," she said. So she started publishing a newsletter that provided her clients with the information she might have left out of her meetings. When company management saw how well the newsletter worked to increase sales in Floyd's territory, they decided to distribute it company-wide and use it as a marketing tool for a dozen salespeople. The company's art department took care of laying it out and typesetting it. However, Floyd later realized she could produce the newsletter for her company much more cheaply on a Macintosh of her own, so the company assigned her that responsibility. Once she had the equipment, she began to look for other newsletter jobs on the side. In a short time, she had a full-fledged business going, and she decided to get out of travel and sales.

Soon she was producing newsletters with four full-time employees for twenty-five clients from mostly high-tech and industrial companies. Unfortunately, she found that she was spending more time managing her employees and the business and less time actually working on the newsletter. When Floyd moved to New Orleans with her husband because of his job promotion, she disbanded her business, and set out to start from scratch again.

In New Orleans, she again started producing newsletters for corporate clients, but was determined to keep her business small this time. She designed a promotional newsletter to tout her services. Although she received some jobs for it, more importantly, she heard from people who wanted to subscribe to her promotional newsletter. After some hesitation, she converted her newsletter into what has grown into *Newsletter News & Resources*, a quarterly eight-page publication for writers, designers, and entrepreneurs who are producing their own newsletters and need some guidance.

Floyd says that the biggest difference between publishing a client newsletter and a subscription newsletter is that people are paying for the information. "I have so much pressure to publish information that's valuable and fresh that it takes me so much longer to do my own newsletter than if it was strictly a marketing piece," she says.

Though she charges $19.95 for a subscription, Floyd still uses the newsletter as a promotional piece for her other products, which have grown to include several books on how to publish a newsletter to promote your own business or somebody else's, and how to use the newsletter to market your business. Her first book, *Marketing with Newsletters*, has sold 13,000 copies through lectures, seminars, bookstores, and mail order. She also thinks about forming a newsletter society where subscribers would purchase a membership and be entitled to a subscription to *Newsletter News & Resources*, a book or two, a directory of newsletter printers, in other words, some information each year.

During her years of producing newsletters—for her own business as well as other companies—Floyd understandably has a lot of advice to give to the aspiring newsletter publisher: "Your topic has to be narrow enough so that it has PR value and you have some kind of a niche, so pick your subject carefully and make sure you know where to find your prospective buyers," she suggests. "Your topic also has to contain a lot of information that is constantly changing and that people have trouble finding on their own. Using my own example, if I were to publish this newsletter as my sole business, it would be tough because it's hard to find newsletter editors."

Since marketing through direct mail is very expensive, Floyd recommends that you pick a subject that subscribers won't hesitate spending money on to get the kind of information they need. The easiest way is to find a real specialized niche of big business that has money to spend. It makes it easier on you because you don't have to go after as many subscribers. "If I could publish a newsletter that costs $199 a year, I'd need only 200 subscribers and I'd be sitting pretty," she says. "With my newsletter, I'd have to have 2,000 subscribers to pull in the same amount of money. New technologies are a good bet for this, as well as any subject that's really hot and that people are really confused about—like the Internet."

Floyd adds that she thinks people get excited about publishing a newsletter because of the possibility of the get-rich-quick aspect. One newsletter that is regularly held up as an example is *The Tightwad Gazette,* which Floyd says is successful because it contains a lot of unusual information in each issue, it's wonderfully written, it's based on a lot of research, and you can tell that the editor Amy Daczyzyn really worked hard on it. "Plus, she's been a real PR queen," says Floyd. "But still, her success didn't happen overnight. Most people don't realize what it takes, and you have to love your subject enough to do it."

8

Newspapers

Description of Business: A company that publishes a weekly, monthly, or quarterly newspaper that focuses on a particular community or area.

Ease of Startup: Moderate. You need to publish a sample issue to demonstrate your newspaper's focus to advertisers.

Range of Initial Investment: $500–$5,000.

Time Commitment: Full-time.

Success Potential: Moderate. This can be successful if there's no competition or if you're addressing a niche that's not being filled.

How to Market the Business: Through radio ads, event sponsorships, adequate distribution, reader contests, and other publicity.

The Pros: Publishing your own newspaper is a way to become the voice of a particular community.

The Cons: Advertisers sometimes pay late or not at all; readers will frequently cancel subscriptions for frivolous reasons.

Special Considerations: For a person with experience in journalism, publishing a newspaper is a power trip. It will get into your blood.

Producing a newspaper is not a common home-based publishing business. The very idea of producing a daily newspaper conjures up images of a noisy, smoky newsroom with harried reporters running around under deadline. But the truth is, specialized newspapers, which are geared toward a specific audience, as well as small, community-based weeklies can be easily handled from the home. One person can handle the editorial from a home computer while another can sell ads. An independent contractor or distribution company should be hired to get the paper out to the public, whether it's free of charge or not.

If you decide to publish a newspaper, you will never have the luxury of time that some other home-based publishing entrepreneurs have, even though they would probably laugh at you if you told them this. With weekly deadlines, or even monthly deadlines, there are no such things as fact checkers or assistants. Basically the story goes into the paper the way it comes into the office, with precious little time to content edit or copyedit.

Why would you publish a newspaper instead of a newsletter or magazine? For one, newsprint is cheaper than the paper used in printing a newsletter or magazine, and it's also a much faster one-feed process, which means you can work much closer to deadline than in any other print publishing format. This lends itself well to publishing a local, community-based weekly paper that tells the news about the schools, senior center, and local businesses.

Profile

Chuck Woodbury
Out West
Grass Valley, California

Like many people, Chuck Woodbury didn't like his job. But unlike most of them, he quit his job and used his savings to travel around the western United States in an RV for two years.

During that time his most pressing decision was whether to turn left, right, or go straight at a congruence of dirt roads out in the middle of nowhere.

He had been working in public relations on a freelance basis for ten years when he decided it was time to bail out. He also had a small monthly newspaper he was publishing, which he sold to finance his bare-bones living expenses for a couple of years.

Somewhere in the middle of Wyoming toward the end of the first year of traveling, he thought of combining his two passions—traveling and writing—into a business he could run himself. Woodbury published the first issue of *Out West* barely six weeks later. Today *Out West* is a quarterly, forty-page newspaper filled mostly with Woodbury's stories about the places he visits and the people he sees.

In the beginning, the paper was twenty-four pages and had twenty-five subscribers—mostly Woodbury's family and friends. After the first issue was published, he sent copies out to the press. Shortly thereafter, the news media started calling. A few months later, he appeared on ABC's *World News Tonight,* and the subscriptions started to pour in.

Despite the power they wield, many members of the media are as unhappy with their jobs as the rest of the world. Chuck feels that the media responded so enthusiastically to *Out West* because there were many journalists who would love to do what he was doing. They naturally felt a lot of their readers would feel the same way. "I was doing something I loved. I was able to make a living from it, but went into it on a shoestring," he says. "Also, I was free. That's why the media wrote about me so much, and that's why people subscribe."

To do the research for an issue, Chuck spends about a month on the road with his wife, Rodica—who serves as associate editor—and their young daughter, Emily. They decide to cover a certain area before they leave; they stick to the less-frequently traveled roads and avoid the interstates.

He writes and designs the newspaper on a Macintosh. On the road he uses a laptop computer, importing the data into the

Macintosh when he gets home. One reason he started the news-paper is because he thought it would be fun; he has to work really hard to keep the business part of the paper under control. "I've been tempted a few times to increase the frequency of the paper to bimonthly, but then everything would become a chore," he says. "Besides, I don't want to hire anybody because then I'd be a boss. I'm more concerned about putting out a good product than spending a lot of time promoting the paper. By putting out a quality product, it promotes itself."

He still sends news releases and sample copies to the media. He does radio talk shows over the phone while he's traveling and when he's at home. "I do about four or five shows a month on big-city radio stations. I phone in from wherever I am. It's a good source of new subscriptions."

Out West accepts advertising, but Woodbury doesn't do much to solicit new ads; as a result, the ratio of editorial to advertising space is about nine to one. The paper grosses about $100,000 a year from subscriptions and ancillary products, such a videotape and a book Chuck wrote for a major publisher. He'd like to spend more time increasing the renewal rate, which stands at 60 percent, but he can only send out a few renewal notices. "I don't like to play that game," he indicates, but many people won't renew until they get a fifth notice, so he's added another mailing.

He writes and lays out the paper before sending it to the printer, who then passes it along to a mailing service. And he maintains his own mailing list. "It's important to keep your overhead really low," he warns. "Don't get carried away with equipment, even though it's easy to become addicted to the new technology."

For people who are thinking about starting their own news-paper, Woodbury has a tip: "Find a subject that's of burning interest to you. With the new technology, it's very easy and af-fordable to get the word out."

9

Software

Description of Business: A company that publishes information in a software program or on computer disk or CD-ROM.

Ease of Startup: Moderate. You don't need to know how to program software; you do need a good idea and the fortitude to market it for the long-term and produce updates when necessary.

Range of Initial Investment: $7,500 for programming fees for a simple program and no fancy packaging; $15,000 and up for something more substantial.

Time Commitment: Part- to full-time.

Success Potential: Moderate. Copycat programs are doomed to failure. You need to produce a program that people will use in their daily lives, but that contains something different from other programs currently on the market.

How to Market the Business: Through direct mail, publicity, sales reps and wholesaling to software stores, and selling in bulk to organizations and businesses.

The Pros: In most cases, you don't need to invest money in keeping a large inventory, since the turnaround time on duplicating programs tends to be brief. Plus, you don't need to be fluent in programming to produce a piece of software.

The Cons: The field is getting crowded; competition from big software companies with extremely deep pockets may mean a long, hard struggle, unless you target the markets that they've neglected.

Special Considerations: The appetite for new software is pretty enormous. As with other types of publishing, focusing on a particular niche will increase your chances of success.

Profile

Lisa Shaw
The Business Traveler's Guide to Inns & B&Bs
Williams Hill Publishing

I produced *The Business Traveler's Guide to Inns & B&Bs* as a Windows-based software program because at the time I couldn't afford to tie up the little money I had in an inventory of books that would go out of date in a year. It also came about because of *Travel Marketing Bulletin*, a newsletter I was publishing eight times a year that told innkeepers and others who ran small travel businesses how to market their businesses more effectively.

I had been kicking around ideas for a B&B directory for some time. There were already many directories in book form, but they were primarily aimed toward leisure travelers. Many of the B&B hosts and innkeepers who I interviewed for articles for *Travel Marketing Bulletin* had asked me to write stories on how they could attract more business travelers to their inns.

I wrote a few stories on how to market to business travelers. Then one day I stumbled upon a great idea (remember to always respect these moments of recognition and creativity!). Why not publish a B&B directory for business travelers? I explained my idea to a woman who ran a trade association for people who owned B&B reservation services. She liked it, but said that since most business travelers use laptops, perhaps I should put it on disk instead of in book form. On disk, I could also update the information instantly, instead of waiting for a book publisher to print a revised edition. Plus, in the beginning I could make copies of the disks on my home computer. If it became too labor intensive, I could farm out the work to a disk duplication service.

I then began to plan the type of information I wanted to include in each listing. I would include the standard stuff—such as the name of the innkeeper and the business, contact information, the credit cards they accept (if any)—as well as special information that would be pertinent to the business traveler market (e.g., can guests use the office equipment at the inn?).

Because I didn't have a lot of money, I didn't want to produce a paper manual to include with each copy of the program or spend time on the phone with people who had technical support questions. The programmer I worked with assured me that even a monkey could install the program and learn to run it.

I provided the programmer with some sample listings and ideas about the format of the program. I wanted a map of the United States to appear on the screen so the user could click on the state in which he or she was looking for an inn, after which an alphabetical list of the inns in that state would pop up. The user could then click on an inn to get more details.

While the programmer worked on the skeleton of the program, I collected my data. I sent questionnaires to 12,000 different inns, B&Bs, and reservation services from a mailing list I had rented. I received just over 750 responses, and farmed out the data entry work to a local college student. Once the list was complete, I sent the information to the programmer, who plugged it into his skeleton program. After spending a few weeks to test for bugs, he sent me a master disk to load onto my computer.

During the time that he was testing the program, I prepared my first batch of promotional mailings. Again, I knew I would begin by marketing directly to consumers, and the first stage involved sending press kits to travel and business media. I could then use the first media articles to get even more publicity, and perhaps to interest a distributor, catalog company, and organizations who would purchase the *Guide* wholesale in bulk.

I knew from researching the business traveler market that women were most likely to stay in an inn or B&B. So I targeted women's publications as well as the standard travel and business magazines. I sent out press kits without a copy of the program, since that would get too expensive. I did invite media writers and editors, however, to call me directly if they wanted to receive a review copy of the program.

The Business Traveler's Guide to Inns & B&Bs was written up in *Entrepreneur, Working Woman, Bottom Line, Frequent Flier, Nation's Business*, and in many newspapers and other magazines during its first year on the market. The first edition has sold approximately 10,000 copies. Since guidebook information can become quickly outdated, I've decided to produce an update every year and perhaps offer more features to the program to appeal to business travelers. And although I sold the program as a free-standing directory the first time around, I have decided to package the program with other materials for the second edition in kit form. I'll call it something like "The Business Traveler's Survival Kit," and it will include a copy of the program, a booklet of tips to help reduce the stress of constant travel, and perhaps a bottle of aspirin.

Though it is gimmicky, this is what will catch the eye of a busy editor and a busy business traveler. I've discovered that if you can make life a little easier for the customer who will purchase your software—or any of the other types of publications described in this book—you will win accolades and lots of orders.

10

Zines

Description of Business: A company that publishes a low-budget, quirky periodical called a zine, which serves more as a forum for the publisher/editor's opinions than as a vehicle for information and advice.

Ease of Startup: Easy. All you need is a typewriter or computer and access to a copy machine.

Range of Initial Investment: $100 and up.

Time Commitment: Part-time

Success Potential: Difficult, if you want to make any money publishing a zine. Easy, if all you want to do is circulate your writing.

How to Market the Business: Over the Internet, through other zines, and by passing them out to friends, family, coworkers, and total strangers.

The Pros: It's easy to start a zine, and if you've always been frustrated by receiving rejection slips from other publications, your troubles will be over.

The Cons: Don't expect to make any money publishing a zine. You'll be lucky to break even.

Special Considerations: Publishing a zine can be great for the ego and create a way for you to be in touch with lots of other people who share your ideas. But be prepared to view your zine as more of a social outlet than a profitable one.

Profile

Kathy Biehl
Ladies' Fetish & Taboo Society Compendium of Urban Anthropology
Houston, Texas

Like many publishers, Kathy Biehl started a zine, called *Ladies' Fetish & Taboo Society Compendium of Urban Anthropology,* because she had some ideas that she wanted to share with her friends as well as with other people. Of course, the version of the zine that she publishes today doesn't much resemble her early efforts.

"It all started in 1988 as a series of photocopied pages of bizarre things that had caught my eye in law journals and in newspapers," she said. She found these items to be so weird that she just had to share them with her friends. At first, she just collected little tidbits of incredibly odd stuff, taped it to pieces of paper, brought it to Kinko's, and ran it through the copy machines before sending it on to friends. The first couple of years, Biehl sent these copies out whenever her drawer full of odd tidbits began to overflow, which happened about once a year.

She says that she started publishing the zine to prove to people that this oddball stuff really happens, and adds that the zine has contained several running themes over the years, such as frustration with bureaucracy and gender confusion. When the publication started to circulate, she received letters from people all over the world. "Complete strangers would write to me, pouring their guts out, telling me about the strange things that had happened to them," she says. "As a result of publishing the zine, I have developed very unusual friendships, and all kinds of people send me strange stories about things they've overheard at the grocery store, or unbelievable things that have happened to them at the bureaucracies where they work." In this way, a lot of Biehl's research for the zine is done for her, though she still contributes a lot of her own experiences to the publication. Each issue of *Ladies' Fetish & Taboo Society Compendium of Urban Anthropology* is sixteen pages, unless Biehl gets way behind schedule. Then she publishes a double issue that contains twenty-four pages. She tries to publish a new issue four times a year, but admits that the official publication schedule is "whenever," and actually states this on her masthead. Such is the flexibility of publishing a zine; you couldn't get away with this if you were publishing a magazine or newsletter, but in the world of zine publishing, it's expected and almost encouraged.

A subscription to *Ladies' Fetish & Taboo Society Compendium of Urban Anthropology* costs $10 for four issues ($14 for subscribers who live outside the United States). Biehl doesn't accept paid advertising, but she will barter advertising for other zines and products that strike her fancy. With no advertising revenue, she must pay her expenses solely from subscriptions; she breaks even with 200 subscribers. Like virtually every zine publisher, Biehl doesn't do it for the money. "I do it as an alternative to therapy," she admits, and adds that since she's worked as a freelance writer since 1982, publishing a zine is the only way to say things that no one else would dare to print. When she started the zine, it cost her only a few dollars; now she spends around $300 on photocopying and another $100 for postage.

Indeed, *Ladies' Fetish & Taboo Society Compendium of Urban Anthropology* is eclectic, cheeky, and well written, but I see where it would go over the heads of many people. Biehl says that a lot of people have written to her to say how much they *hate* her zine. "It's very quirky," she says. "You have to read the print zine fairly closely, but by the end of an issue it all starts to make sense." She describes her audience as ranging in age from their mid-twenties to mid-forties, and extremely well read. Though they're mostly college educated, they tend to be overeducated and underemployed. "I've never run a survey of my readers, but there seem to be certain themes that they have in common, which include a good knowledge of classical music and a familiarity with gay and alternative lifestyles, though it is not a gay publication," says Kathy.

Her renewal rate on the zine hovers around 65 percent, so to keep the zine going, she must constantly scout for new readers. She trades subscriptions with other zine publishers, expecting that some of the other zines will review *Ladies' Fetish & Taboo Society Compendium of Urban Anthropology,* and that their readers will subscribe. She also sends a subscription to a publication called *Factsheet Five,* which is considered the mother of all zines. "It's a zine that exists to review zines and other small publications with thumbnail listings of anything they think has merit," she explains. "It's published twice a year, and, in fact, I get most of my requests for sample issues through *Factsheet Five.*"

She also promotes her zine by reprinting excerpts from the publication on her Web site, but she is opposed to placing each complete issue there because it's very easy for anybody to steal her work. She says that one of the best things she's ever written, an essay called "101 Ways to Sabotage Your Date," had been downloaded and sent to a humor Usenet group. The members of that group then circulated the essay over the Internet, which can reach tens of thousands of people in a matter of hours. Biehl was unaware that her work was being circulated until a subscriber stumbled upon a few cases where people had downloaded her essay and passed it off as their own. As a result, she is very selective about what she will place on the Web.

Another way that she promotes her zine is through an electronic newsletter called *Demitasse,* which contains articles and teasers that Biehl doesn't plan to publish in the zine. "It's a blatant pitch for people to subscribe," she admits. She also spends lots of time surfing the Internet. Anytime that she finds a Web page that is particularly well written and might attract the type of people who would appreciate her zine, and it has a site that reviews other publications, she'll send a note to the Webmaster asking them to visit her page and consider including it on their review site.

Besides freelancing writing, Biehl is also a self-employed attorney, which is the reason why she considers her publication schedule to be "whenever." And since she views her zine as a way to get her thoughts out into the world, and not as a way to make money, she isn't pressured by the bottom line like other publishers.

Often it seems that zine publishers exist solely to communicate with other zine publishers. "In the underground publishing world, there is a vast network of people who are involved in producing zines to varying degrees, and a lot of us end up in communication with each other through the mail and e-mail," says Kathy. "We frequently trade things back and forth, and give each other ideas and sometimes leads, though this field of publishing doesn't seem to have the element of cutthroatness to it that other forms do."

In the past, Biehl's zine has been sold on a wholesale level through a distributor and has appeared on bookstore and magazine shelves, but she admits that it doesn't have a tremendous amount of shelf appeal. "It does contain some graphics," she says, "but it doesn't have a glossy cover and it's not splashy at all." In fact, her zine is very text heavy, which, in a sense, is expected because she's deliberately parodying academic style.

Biehl intends to keep her quirky publication in the form of a zine. "I wouldn't want to do it as a magazine because it would cost more and I don't have the time," she says. "With this kind of format you can get away with an awful lot. The content to me is more important than the way that I present it, though I do want it to look tidy. Some zine publishers will paste stuff together, reproduce images, make collages, and play with their graphics programs, but I don't have the time to spare."

Biehl comments on two disadvantages to publishing a zine: "First, you are not going to make any money at it and you're lucky if you break even," she says. "Secondly, by publishing a zine, you open yourself up to some pretty nasty criticism. It's astonishing, the zine world is like any social group and there are cliques and people who take it upon themselves to pass judgment on other people. I have received some phenomenally vicious reviews and I never did anything to these people, and you can get your ego bent out of shape if you take it seriously."

But she'll continue to publish, both for the joy of getting her words out into the world and for the feedback and encouragement that she receives from kindred spirits who are far, far away. "It makes you feel a lot less alone," she says.

PART THREE

The Business of Running Your Home-Based Publishing Business

11

Defining Your Home-Based Publishing Business

Once you start to narrow down what kind of home-based publishing business you want to start, it's a good idea to have all of the broad strokes confirmed so you can start planning the details before you begin.

If you haven't yet narrowed down the type of publishing business you'd like to run, or if you can't decide between several of the ideas you have for a business, it's a good idea to write out plans for each of them. Sometimes, just seeing the specifics down in black and white may help you to make your final decision. And keep in mind that some of your answers to these questions will become more refined as you continue reading this book.

Refine Your Idea

You may have already decided on the type of publishing business you'd like to run. Great—the next thing you need to do is refine your idea, check out your competition, and put your own unique spin on the topic.

My point in taking you through this step-by-step process is to make sure that your home-based publishing business will

serve a particular market that is being neglected and is relatively easy to reach. I feel that these are the first issues that any
entrepreneur should address before starting a new business.

During the course of your research, if you discover that a
competitor has already beaten you to your idea, just twist your
idea some more: either slant it towards another market, or specialize in a particular group of people or businesses. For instance,
if someone is already publishing a newsletter about how doctors can utilize the Internet and World Wide Web to market
their businesses, you can go after lawyers, restaurants, or flo-
rists. Focusing on a particular group will make it easier to succeed
than if you focus broadly on any business owner that can market with the Internet.

To begin, use a notebook and sketch out the details of your
home-based publishing business by asking yourself the following questions:

- What kind of publishing business would I be happy with?
  (Be as specific as possible.)
- Can I run it full-time or part-time while I keep my
  present job?
- When do I want to start my business?
- How much time do I need to plan my business?
- How can my friends and family help me?
- How much money do I need to start my business?
- How do I think I'm going to spend the majority of my
  time when I'm working on my business?

Do Your Homework

Overall, no matter what type of publishing business you want
to start, research is quite critical to the potential success of your
business.

In time, you may discover that once you've researched and
planned what you're going to do, you'll see that you do indeed
have the courage to go ahead with it, which is something that

even entrepreneurs who have been in business for decades still experience. Many people check out absolutely everything, from the geographic location of their businesses to taking specialized classes in their field as well as lining up mentors to turn to for feedback. This last step also ensures that you'll have a ready network of supportive people before you take the big leap.

How Much Time Do You Need to Plan Your Home-Based Publishing Business?

Some people will decide what kind of home-based publishing business they want to run and then jump right in that same day, week, or month. Most people need a little more time. Deciding how much time you're going to need to plan your business is not an exact science; it depends on you. Some people plan for three months when they could have benefited more from six months, while others who took a year find that they could have started marketing their business and soliciting customers after only six months of planning.

The amount of time you need to plan your home-based publishing business primarily depends on your financial situation and the faith you have in your abilities. If you need to plan every little detail in order to feel confident enough to start a business, then you should take up to a year or more to plan it. But if you feel that the longer you put it off, the more likely that running your own business will just remain a good idea, and not reality, then by all means, do whatever is necessary to get your affairs in order, and then plunge right in, perhaps only after a couple of months of planning.

What Will Your Home-Based Publishing Business Look Like?

It's difficult to know exactly what running your home-based publishing business will be like until you actually begin. But once you start planning, it's likely that you will have a clearer picture of what you're going to be doing. In your notebook, write down your thoughts and actions to the following questions:

- What are some of the expectations that you have about the business you've chosen?
- Are you prepared to switch gears if your business starts to disappoint you? How do you think you'll do it?
- What external motivations will you set up to keep you going?
- Brainstorm: Write down a schedule of the perfect day running your business.

What are your impressions of entrepreneurial life? If you're like most people who are interested in starting a home-based publishing business, having control over your life, making some money, and pursuing your favorite activity are probably at the top of your list. I'd bet money that the main reason you want to start your own business is because your present life contains none of those things. Obviously, you think that running your own business would eliminate some of the biggest pains in your life while creating several new ones that you've never had to deal with before.

However, some people start their own home-based publishing businesses not because they have a burning desire to be an entrepreneur, but because they hate their current lives. These are the people who tend not to last more than two years in their own businesses before they turn right around and close their businesses and get a full-time job working for somebody else again.

Be Realistic

To put it bluntly, starting your own home-based publishing business is about changing your entire life. That's why it's important to be realistic about why you want to become an entrepreneur in the first place. The first step is to deal with the fact that you're leaving your seemingly secure, predictable life behind you. In my experience, the number one reason why people don't start their own businesses when they really want to is because they think they won't make any money at it. The number two reason concerns security: Even though you may hate your present life, after all, it's all you know and it's familiar. Though you may have developed your mental image of entrepreneurial life from the many articles and TV shows that tout the advantages of the lifestyle—usually without ever mentioning any of the disadvantages, I might add—you probably still are not clear on what it will be like for you. Will you be able to make it? Will you be able to pay the bills? Whatever is holding you back, it's likely that one or all of these concerns are major issues for you.

So before you begin to dream about the kind of business you'd like to run or what your daily life will be like, take some time to figure out *why* you want to change your life.

Everyone has their own reasons for wanting to run their own business. However, if you're not clear about these reasons before you start—and if you do it for what I think of as the wrong reasons—you may discover that once you become responsible for your own publishing business that you won't want to put up with the tough stuff, since you had no idea what to expect.

Try as you want to view a move into entrepreneurial self-sufficiency as an instant metamorphosis that transforms your life into everything you've ever wanted, you must realize that many of your old problems will still be around. It's the same type of thing whenever a woman says or believes that if she could only lose that last ten pounds, then life would be perfect: "If I could only quit my job and start my own business, my life will magically change for the better." Though there are some pragmatic people who don't subscribe to this philosophy, I know that many people do. Therefore, the clearer your reasons for what you hope to accomplish by starting your own business, the more successful your transition into entrepreneurial life will be.

In your notebook, write the answers to the following questions to help you to get clear about the *why* behind your decision to strike out on your own. Even though you may already have a good idea of why you want to start your own business, answering the following questions will help you to focus in on your true motivations. Answer the following questions honestly and go into as much detail as you need. And keep your answers in mind as you continue to read.

- Why do you want to start your own home-based publishing business? Give five reasons and rank them in order of importance.
- What do you want to know how to do after you've been running your publishing business for a year? How do you propose to learn about it?
- Describe your fantasy publishing business and everything about it.
- What do you like about your current job?
- What do you hate about your current job?
- What do you want to learn in the process of starting your own business?
- What could you do today to bring you one step closer to running your home-based publishing business?
- What's your biggest excuse for *not* starting your business today?

Brainstorm: Quickly make a list of fifty things that you associate with being an entrepreneur. Think about how they'll fit into your life once you start your home-based publishing business. Write them down even if they make no sense. Then cross out the half that are less important. Take the remaining twenty-five and ponder their place in your life and whether they fall under the category of fantasy, reality, or a little of both.

Visualizing Your Home-Based Publishing Business

Now is the perfect time to try to visualize your home-based publishing business. You may want to answer these questions twice: once for how you view your business when you're first starting out, and again a year or more later, after you are able to gain some experience and perspective about what it's really like to run a business, and when you're able to get a clearer idea about your plans for the future. If you're starting your business with a partner, both of you should separately fill out this form and compare your answers. If any of your answers are radically different, you should address them now to avoid disagreements later.

- What will you name your company?
- What will be your primary product or service? What will be some secondary services?
- Will you devote yourself to your business full- or part-time? If part-time, how long will you run it in this way?
- What type of people will use what you have to sell?
- Describe the overall tone of your business: lush and expensive, or spartan?
- How and where will you market your business?
- What will make your business stand out?
- Who are your competitors? How will your business be different?

Writing Your Business Plan

Why should you have a business plan? By this time, you probably have some idea about what kind of home-based publishing business you want to run and when you will start. Even if your goals are not that specific at this point, you probably know that you would rather publish books than a magazine, for example.

Writing a business plan will help you to map out a specific blueprint to follow on your way to meeting your business goals. A business plan addresses even the smallest aspect of getting your business off the ground; in the confusion and excitement of being a new entrepreneur, after all, many things get overlooked. Getting it all down in writing beforehand will provide you with a detailed itinerary. And since you write the plan yourself, you'll be able to tailor it to your own needs, and also to tinker with it later when unforeseen roadblocks emerge.

With a business plan in hand, you'll be able to show the bank, your suppliers, and other potential business contacts exactly how you visualize your business, in language and figures they understand. But writing is a funny thing that reveals a lot as it unfolds. Not only will your business plan provide you with a broad picture of your business, allowing you to get all of the little details down in writing, but in writing it you'll confront many aspects of your prospective business that might not have come up otherwise.

Having a business plan written before you do anything else for your business will put you way ahead of your competition, since most businesses do not take the time beforehand to plan out their strategies as carefully. I know—sometimes I haven't written a business or marketing plan before starting a business, and I paid for it down the road when I became unfocused about exactly what I wanted to accomplish. It's never too late to write a business plan.

Although a business plan is vital to the successful startup of a business, you shouldn't tuck it away in a drawer and forget about it. It is meant to be used and referred to as you progress in your home-based publishing business. Periodically checking the progress you're making against the goals you put forth in the plan allows you to see where changes need to be made, as well as seeing whether you're keeping up with, or even surpassing, your original goals.

As I've mentioned, one of the top reasons why businesses fail is due to a lack of planning. Writing a detailed business plan that is geared towards your ideal will let you see if your goals fit in with your budget, if you should wait until you've raised more money, or indeed, if this is the right type of publishing business for you after all.

Anyone who reads your business plan will be able to get a clear picture of the type of business you want to run, as well as its projected financial health. Spend the time on it now—if you run into trouble later on and don't have a business plan to refer back to, it just might be too late.

Sample Business Plan

A business plan can be only a few pages long, or a massive 100-page document that maps out every single detail involved in running your home-based publishing business.

Though it takes more time, it's best to err on the side of quantity when writing a business plan. The more you know about your publishing business before your first customer walks through the door or calls on the phone, the better prepared you will be for the surprises that will inevitably arise.

A business plan should have five sections: A cover sheet, your statement of purpose for the business, and a table of contents. Then, the meaty part: Section One describes the business—what you provide; your target markets; your location, competition, and personnel you expect to hire. Section Two concerns financial information about the business: Income and cash flow projections, and if you're buying a business from another owner, and the financial history of the business as they ran it.

Another section of your business plan should consist of supporting documents that back up the information you're providing in the other sections. A resume of your employment history, a copy of your credit report, letters of reference, and any other items you believe will help the reader to better grasp what you are striving to do with your business.

For an example of a business plan, see Appendix 1, page 203.

Starting a Home-Based Publishing Business from Scratch

If you decide to start your business from scratch, you will need to do more work in the beginning than if you bought an existing business. The advantage of starting your own business is that it costs less; it will also bear your personal stamp from the outset. Buying someone else's business means that you'll have to work within a successful format and style that may not fit your own. You'll have to tinker with the formula slowly—and even then, you may lose customers. Another disadvantage is that it will take more time before the money starts to come in steadily. You will also need to work hard on developing and building your reputation. There's also a lot more detail and legal work to do if you start from scratch.

The main disadvantage to starting a business from scratch is that you won't have income from the business until you start attracting customers, which usually takes longer than your initial estimates. In fact, while you do pay more at the outset for an existing business, the business can start producing revenue for you on the day you take over, since once you assume ownership, you also keep any new business and revenue that comes in after the transfer of ownership. You should weigh the pros and cons against your own temperament before you proceed with buying an existing business. However, I find that the vast majority of home-based publishing entrepreneurs start their own businesses from scratch because the type of product they want to produce doesn't exist.

If you buy an existing business, most of the business technicalities have already been set up for you, from registering your business name to handling insurance for your business—though you do have to change everything over into your name.

If you decide to purchase an existing business instead of starting your own, you have the advantage of having a track record by which you can compare your own efforts, though you still need to write a business and marketing plan.

Buying an established publishing business means that you probably have the advantage of a good reputation and a well-developed list of loyal customers. Sometimes, buying an existing business will actually cost less than starting from scratch if you factor in the reputation of the business, the customer list, computer equipment, and other amenities that are included in the purchase price. And if you figure that your labor is worth something, even though you probably won't be paying yourself a salary for quite some time, buying a business outright may turn out to be a veritable bargain.

I sold a newsletter I had been publishing for a couple of years to the company that was handling my circulation duties. When the buyer's lawyer sent me the first contract to arrange the sale, there was a clause that stated that after the sale transpired, I would be responsible for refunding money to customers who canceled their subscriptions. My lawyer struck the clause from the contract, and the buyer accepted it without a whimper. It's a good thing that we did remove the clause, because after the new owner took over and completely changed the direction of the business, it folded after only two issues.

12

Getting Your Home-Based Publishing Business off the Ground

Every one of the details and aspects that are involved in starting your home-based publishing business will probably serve as the proving ground of your enterprise: After all, if you're still enthusiastic about your business after you've gotten through all the grunt work that's necessary to get it up and running, then you know you've made the right decision.

Even if you've fallen slightly out of love with your field of endeavor after the startup tasks, you shouldn't worry, because the moment you make your first sale or hold a copy of your first published book in your hands, all the reasons why you wanted to start your own publishing business will come rushing back at you.

You just have to jump through a few hoops first.

Naming Your Publishing Business

Many people name their publishing businesses after themselves. This works if you're a consulting firm, but not if you're a one-person business just starting out, if you're the only one answering your business phone line. Some entrepreneurs use their initials—such as LAN Enterprises—but, again, I don't feel that this says anything.

Since you'll probably want to expand your business somewhere down the road, which may include new products and services that may or may not be related to what you're doing now, you should give your publishing business a name that conveys that the sky's the limit as far as your future business is concerned. That is, you need to think broadly and imagine the variety of publications—books, magazines, software—that you may be producing in just a few short years. Therefore, you should pick a relatively nondescript name for your business that is able to encompass all future projects as well as convey a professional image to customers *now*.

Pick a name that is amorphous, a name that means something personally to you, and that sends a certain professional message about your business. I'll use my own business—Williams Hill Publishing—as an example.

When I started publishing *Sticks*, my fourth newsletter, in the spring of 1994, I needed to choose a company name. In the past, I've looked to local geographical maps as well as other local businesses for ideas. In my area, there are at least five businesses named after Moose Mountain, a geographical landmark that is located a few towns away from me. That sounded good as a company name for *Sticks*, I surmised, and so I decided that it would serve as my business name. I also knew I would be starting up another newsletter two months later, so the title seemed to be a good fit.

Until I went to register my business name with the state, that is, which promptly informed me that the name was already taken. (Of course, I had already bullheadedly ignored all the advice in every single business book that told me to register a business name with the state before printing up stationery, checks, etc. My bank was very trusting: They assumed that I had already done my homework and never asked to see my business certificate. But when I went back to change the name several months later, they *did* ask to see it.) Although it was a bit of a pain, part of me was glad I had to change it, since to me and my associates' ears, Moose Mountain did sound a bit hickish, not an image I wanted my business to portray over the long haul.

So, the second time around, I got out the local maps again. I rejected Half-Moon Press, after a local pond (some might say it sounded half-baked), Grafton Press (I might move), and Cardigan Mountain Publishing (too close to another publisher, Cadogan Guides). A nearby road caught my eye—actually a road I planned to buy land on—and Williams Hill Publishing was born. I chose *Publishing* instead of *Press* because *Press* sounds like it limits itself to printed matter, and I knew I wanted to pursue other publishing projects in the future. The name was suitably professional, I had a personal connection to it, and my current and future projects both fit well into it.

Here's how I named two of my newsletters: *Sticks* just popped into my head one morning while I was thinking about derogatory names for the country, but another newsletter called *Travel Marketing Bulletin* was more specifically crafted.

There was already a newsletter with the name *Travelwriter Marketletter*, and another by the name of *Inn Marketing*. According to my spies, a home-based publishing business by the name of *Successful Hotel Marketer* was about to go belly-up, which would be useful later on when I was scouting for writers.

My newsletter would show inns, B&Bs, outfitters, travel bureaus, and other small travel businesses how to better market themselves with lots of case histories, tips, and ideas. I basically knew I wanted to use *Travel* and *Marketing*, but I wasn't sure about anything else. I looked at other newsletters, some of which used *News* and *Notes* in their titles, both of which I hated. I typed them into the computer anyway, and used the thesaurus function. *Bulletin* popped out at me.

If you're having trouble choosing a name, go back to one of the business directories and flip through the listings for businesses whose topics have nothing to do with yours. Ask yourself how your business will help your customers. If you can, try to incorporate that angle into your business name, as well as in the titles of the individual publications you will produce.

Your Home-Based Publishing Business and the Law

With any business, whether or not it involves publishing, there are certain legal restrictions that you have to meet in order to do business. The first thing you need to do is register your business with your state government. There will be a fee for this, and the purpose is to make sure no other business is currently operating with your name. If there is, you will have to find another name for your business.

Registration will also alert the state to expect tax revenue from your business. If you don't file a state income tax return with your state tax authorities each year, they'll know where to find you. When you register with the state, you should also ask about other regulations you have to meet in order to operate as a home business in your state. Most of the time, they will refer you to your own city government, which is responsible for determining zoning and other business regulations, since it will collect the fees from any permits for renovations that you will need to do.

The important thing at this point is to find out what departments the state, city, or county are each responsible for, the type of registration you will have to make with each, and to make sure you comply with all of them. If you neglect any of the steps necessary to open and operate a business, government authorities at any level have the power to shut it down and/or do whatever is necessary to bring your business into compliance. The time to find all of this out is before you open your doors. So it pays to do your homework first.

You'll also need to determine the form of business you'll run: a sole proprietorship, partnership, or a corporation. Each has its advantages and disadvantages, and home-based business owners have very specific reasons for picking one over the others.

Sole Proprietorship

A sole proprietorship is the form of business that most single-owner businesses pick. It's easy to start—all you have to do is register with the state and you're in business—you make all the decisions yourself, and except for zoning concerns (if you're running your business from your home), you're pretty much free from having to follow complex laws regarding the operation of your business. You alone are responsible for the success or failure of your business, and any profits that your business earns are reported as income in your name.

With sole proprietorship, legal or financial troubles fall entirely on your shoulders. For many home-based publishing entrepreneurs, liability insurance that's tied in with your business or homeowners policy will often be enough to handle a "reasonable" lawsuit and settlement. The remote chances of being hit with a lawsuit, and the relative ease of operating this form of business ownership, make a sole proprietorship the preferred method of business organization for most home-based publishing entrepreneurs.

However, if your business should fail, you will be responsible for all outstanding debts incurred during the course of doing business. If you don't pay them, or declare bankruptcy, it will be reflected on your personal credit record.

Partnerships

A partnership is actually two sole proprietorships combined into one. This means that while the strengths are doubled, so are the inherent weaknesses.

The most common instance in which an entrepreneur decides to create a partnership is when he or she chooses to enter the business with a friend or business partner. Married couples also sometimes decide to form a partnership when they start a business together. Though a partnership usually means that twice

as much energy and money is available than in a sole proprietorship, if you're thinking about forming a partnership, you
should consider it very carefully before you proceed. The best
partnerships work when the partners have differing but comple-
mentary talents, when each partner does what they do best. For
instance, one partner may have a strong background in marketing and day-to-day business operations, while the other loves
nothing more than to research different markets and report the
results, which the other can use to define the market. As long as
both partners trust each other to concentrate on their own department, and to interfere only when problems arise, then the
partnership will probably do well.

Partnerships usually run into trouble when the partners have
similar skills and/or different ideas about the right way to run a
business. For example, when both partners want to concentrate on sales, but neither wants the behind-the-scenes tasks
such as bookkeeping and managing the office, there are going
to be problems right from the start.

As with a sole proprietorship, if someone decides to sue the
business, usually for libel or defamation, both partners will be
personally liable. And if the business fails, leaving outstanding
debts, again, both partners will be responsible. If one partner
disappears after a business fails, the other must pay all debts.
Be aware of this, because it does happen from time to time.

Corporations

A corporation is best defined as a entity that is treated as a person in the eyes of the law. It is a business organization that has
its own needs aside from those of the business, which include
financial and legal restrictions. It's more difficult, expensive, and
time-consuming to form and operate your business as a corporation, but it also shields you from personal responsibility in
case business sours or a customer decides to sue.

One advantage that a corporation has over a partnership or
sole proprietorship is that it can raise money by selling shares

in the business; when the other two kinds of businesses need cash, they have to borrow money from a bank or from friends. But, remember, a corporation is also constrained by its responsibility to these shareholders, who are really part-owners. Some expansion and growth issues, for example, require the approval of shareholders before the corporation can proceed.

The IRS taxes corporations differently from sole proprietorships and partnerships, and there are even more rules and regulations a corporation must follow on both the state and federal level. There are also certain restrictions on the types of businesses that can be incorporated.

Some publishing entrepreneurs automatically opt for incorporation to protect their personal assets in the case of a lawsuit, and this is prudent. However, the type of business that will benefit most from incorporation is when there are more than two owners controlling the future of the business. With multiple partners deciding the fate of the business, issues of ownership and decision making necessarily become more complex, so it becomes easier to rely on a board of directors and group of stockholders, especially since they've invested their money and trust in the business.

Do You Need an Attorney?

Whether or not you choose to use the services of an attorney to help you set up your home-based publishing business depends on how you view the legal profession as well as how detail-oriented you are. Some publishing entrepreneurs swear by their lawyers and consult with them about every decision they make. Others swear *at* them, and will never use an attorney for anything in their business or personal lives.

The happy medium is somewhere in between. If you're planning to incorporate your business, you'll probably need to use a lawyer, although more people are learning how to incorporate themselves. The vast majority use a lawyer to help facilitate the process, and because their minds are elsewhere.

If, however, you're buying an established publishing business, you will undoubtedly have to hire an attorney to negotiate the terms of the contract. But aside from this, you will probably be able to do most of the tasks involved in starting your business without a lawyer.

Do You Need an Accountant?

If you're unsure about the type of business organization that suits you best—sole proprietorship, partnership, or corporation—it's a good idea to consult with an accountant to help you decide. An accountant will analyze your current financial situation and help you determine what you want to gain from your business in terms of revenue—equity or income—and advise you about how to best achieve your goals.

An accountant can also analyze the books and financial records of a publishing business that you're thinking about buying. It's a good idea to find an accountant who has some experience keeping the books for small companies in your field; you may want to ask small businesses in your area for the names of some accountants they'd recommend. Then call each of them up and interview them before you settle on one.

An accountant can also help you set up a realistic budget and a schedule of projected revenues. And if this is the first time you've run a business of your own, an accountant can also help you become familiar with different accounting methods, tax rates based on projected revenue, and the tax codes of your state, as well as recommend methods of bookkeeping that will make the job easier when tax season rolls around.

Licenses and Permits

Before you conduct business, you must check with the local, county, and state business authorities to find out about the various kinds of licenses and permits you'll need, if any.

Let me explain the purpose of the licenses and permits you will be required to get. Bear in mind, however, these requirements will vary from place to place. States and regions with more highly regulated governments tend to be pickier about what you can and cannot do with your home-based publishing business, and what fees they charge you for the privilege of making enough money to pay taxes.

Even though you may resent all the legalese and paperwork, it's important to meet all of the requirements. No one says you can't complain every step of the way, however.

- You'll need a sales tax certificate from the state to collect tax on any in-state mail-order purchases your customers will make from you.
- Even if your home and facilities meet all of the above regulations, if they are not in an area zoned for business use, you may need to move to an area that's especially zoned for commercial use. It's your town government that determines zoning, and it's also their responsibility to make exceptions to the rules when small businesses are located outside of commercial zones. Even though your business will provide a tax base for your town and help bring money to the local economy, if you have a commercial enterprise operating in a residential area, you will probably still have to apply for a zoning variance.

The rules get creative, though. Some towns will allow you to operate your business at home as long as you don't hang out a sign. You may also have to expand your driveway and parking area to accommodate an increased number of cars.

And far more interesting laws governing small businesses in your area undoubtedly exist. That's why it's important to check all of the requirements *before* you do anything.

Estimating Operating Costs

Operations—the day-to-day routine you set up to maintain some semblance of organization and to help you efficiently run your home-based publishing company—is, admittedly, not one of the most fun or creative parts of your business. In fact, I'll be the first to admit it: Operations can be downright boring.

But running your daily operations in a haphazard way is the quickest way to drive your business right into the ground. Take some time beforehand to set daily operations policy; later on, you'll have more time for the fun stuff.

Every business has its cycles when business is booming and when it is slow. Unfortunately, there are a certain number of business expenses that continue to accrue regardless of cycles; they don't care that you haven't received a check for payment for two weeks; they still demand to be paid.

Running a small business is no exception. In my experience, it will take about six months of constant marketing and promotion before you can expect to see steady revenue flowing into your business; it takes that long for your product to register in the minds of prospective customers. And as I've also said, some people will need to hear about your business more than a few times before they can even think about responding to your offer. So consider yourself forewarned.

There are also several times during the year that are notorious for being slow if you focus on using direct mail for a marketing campaign, especially for a business selling self-improvement products. One of these is the summertime, usually a time for your customers to lounge and enjoy life. Another slow time is December, a time of year when people are preoccupied with the holidays. The idea of enjoying themselves and putting off any self-improvement programs until after New Year's is usually the rule, rarely the exception. So be sure to put away some money ahead of time to get you through these slow times.

If you are purchasing an established business, estimating your operating costs will be easy. Just ask the current owners for the last three years' breakdown of expenses along with the current income statement. If possible, go through the expenses with the owners and ask about the budgeted amounts versus actual expenses. If you are starting from scratch, it will be a little more difficult to estimate your operating costs, but you can still give it a shot. Be aware, however, that most entrepreneurs who are just starting out greatly underestimate their expenses. You may want to ask other entrepreneurs in your field what they spend on certain fixed expenses each month, as well as some of their highest bills. Some people will think you're too nosy and will either give you inaccurate figures on purpose or none at all. Another good way to estimate your operating costs is to contact the suppliers you'll be dealing with. They will probably be very helpful, especially if it looks like you'll be spending significant amounts of money with them in the future.

The following chart contains all possible expenses you may encounter in running your business. I won't provide estimates, since they can vary widely depending on your early goals in terms of promotion and marketing, whether you will work at home or outside, whether you hire help, and so on. You can also use this chart to see which categories you can cut back on or even eliminate entirely. It's a good idea to chart the expenses for each month for a year.

Keeping Good Records

Once you're generating regular income in your home-based publishing business, it's important to keep track of your expenses and revenue sources. On the one hand, it will make things easier for you at tax time, but it's also enlightening to figure out how much money—and time—you could save at the end of the year by farming the work out to another business or independent contractor.

There are as many ways to keep records as there are businesses out there. Some rely on a standard spreadsheet computer program specially designed to help keep track of several different kinds of revenue and expenses, while some stuff receipts in shoe boxes and dump them out at the end of the year, leaving their accountant to handle all of their dirty work.

No matter which method you choose, however, you should make it easy and organize it so you can do it immediately instead of saving up the work to be done in one unmanageable lump at the end of the week. If you're like most entrepreneurs, you'll

Annual Business Expenses

	Jan	Feb	March	April
Overhead				
Mortgage/rent				
Taxes				
Insurance				
Utilities				
Heat				
Office Expenses				
Telephone				
Separate fax line				
Credit card commissions				
Postage				
Stationery supplies				
Printing				
Advertising				
Mailing list rentals				
Mailing house services				
Consultants				
Miscellaneous marketing fees				
Trade show booth rentals				
Trade association dues and memberships				
Accountant and attorney fees				
Contract employees and freelance writers, editors, and designers				
Computer equipment				
Software				
Company Vehicle Expenses				
Loan				
Registration				
Insurance				
Gas				
Employee Expenses				
Payroll				
Taxes				
Insurance				
Workers' compensation				
Bonuses				
Discounts				

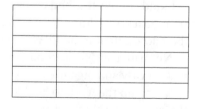

May	June	July	Aug	Sept	Oct	Nov	Dec

Note: For your home-based business, figure your business share of each type of expense, according to the percentage of space your office occupies as a percentage of the square footage of the entire house.

discover how difficult it is to find an uninterrupted block of time anywhere in your week, unless it's in the wee hours of the night.

And in the unlikely case of a tax audit somewhere down the road, it will undoubtedly help boost your case if you can show the auditor receipts that provide answers to all of his questions. Keeping good records will also help you figure out which deductions you'll be able to take.

Good record keeping also helps you track your peak and slow times, as well as knowing where each customer heard about your publishing business and your products. This is important when you start to plan future marketing campaigns. If you know which ad or promotion brought in the largest number of customers this year, then you can concentrate your marketing in the same places next year.

Overall, keeping adequate records just makes good common sense. At the very least, you should get a ledger to organize your records. Some business checking accounts now offer a shortcut in the form of a built-in ledger that allows you to break down the checks you write into different expense categories, which eliminates the need for a separate ledger.

Accounting Basics

Once you start your business, you need to keep track of revenue coming in and expenses going out. It's a good idea to set up an accounting system that works best for you and your business.

There are two kinds of accounting you can use to track revenue and expenses. One is cash accounting, and it involves simple bookkeeping in which income is recorded when it is received, and expenses recorded when bills are paid, even if the expense was incurred in a different month. For instance, say a customer purchases $50 worth of your books on the last day of a month. You deposit her check or charge her purchase to her credit card, the same day, but the income is not posted in your account until a few days later, which happens to fall in the next month. With cash accounting, you record the revenue in the month that you actually received the money into your checking account, and not when the sale was made, which may give you an inaccurate picture of your business cycles if you rely on revenue alone to show the health of your business, and not your month-to-month sales rate. Cash accounting, however, is a very simple way to keep your books, and many home-based publishing entrepreneurs prefer it for its simplicity.

Accrual accounting is more painstaking in its execution, but it gives a more accurate view of revenue and expenses, and of your monthly financial situation. Even though payment may be received or credited the following month—and expenses paid on a net-thirty system since the expenses occurred in the previous month—they are recorded in that month's ledgers, and not when they were actually paid.

When drawing up your accounting sheets, no matter which method you choose, refer to the categories named in the previous section, Estimating Operating Costs. You may want to list certain expenses in categories that are even more specific. Again, bear in mind the method and categories that will work best for your business.

Hiring Employees

Some publishing entrepreneurs prefer to keep their operations as small, one-person businesses, specifically so they'll be able to handle all the jobs themselves without having to hire outside help. Hiring and managing employees adds a whole new dimension to your business and has both its good and bad points: For one, it means more paperwork because you'll have to pay state, federal, and perhaps local payroll taxes in addition to Social Security and workers' compensation, and insurance—that is, if you decide to offer it. On the other hand, having someone around to help out with the grunt work means you'll have more time to focus on running and building your business, like marketing and exploring new services to provide to your growing customer base.

But unfortunately, a common complaint of business owners everywhere today is that it's hard to find good help; after all, no paid employee is going to regard your business and customers in the same way you do. So you'll probably have to lower your standards of quality and attention and plan to spend some time picking up the slack.

And with the rise in unlawful sexual harassment suits brought as the result of being fired, many small business owners have been further discouraged from hiring help, even though they may want to.

Many entrepreneurs advise that if you find an employee who is the exception to the rule, hold onto her or him as tightly as you can by increasing pay, offering bonuses, and showing your appreciation by adding responsibilities or agreeing to the occasional day off with pay.

When hiring employees, there are certain things you have to do. If you're hiring someone to work for you regularly—answering the phone, running errands, and dealing with customers—that person will be considered your employee. You will be responsible for deducting taxes from that person's paycheck, which should be filed with the government either quarterly or once a year, depending on your tax setup.

Some businesses get around the process of withholding and payroll taxes by hiring an employee as an independent contractor. With this arrangement, the contractor files a self-employment tax, which saves you a lot of paperwork. This works for such seasonal and periodic workers as gardeners and musicians, but it will send up red flags with the IRS if you try to hire a part-time office assistant in this way. If you hire an independent contractor and pay them more than $600 over the course of a year, you must file a 1099 form on their behalf, which reports their income.

No matter how you decide to "hire" an employee, make sure that you always communicate with them clearly, directly, and immediately if there's a problem or complaint. And let them know you appreciate a job well done.

Working with Suppliers

When you're first starting out, you'll probably buy your supplies—stationery, computer equipment, and office supplies—from stores and businesses you already have dealt with in the past. Later on, as you grow, you might want to deal directly with wholesalers, commercial distributors, mailing houses, and larger printers. Even if you do reach that point, you still might prefer to do it all yourself by working with a smaller printer who costs more but is a ten-minute drive away, or by hiring a part-time assistant to help out in a crunch.

The first issue you'll face when approaching suppliers is that they usually require large minimum orders so that they can keep their costs down. For instance, instead of ordering 10 boxes of copy paper, you may have to buy 100. Obviously, even if your per-unit cost is half the regular price, you may not want to tie up a lot of money in copy paper, not to mention the overhead that's necessary to store it. The surprise may come when you compare the prices of the larger supplier with your small local store: You may discover that the big company's prices are actually higher than the local store, since the big guys may include the cost of delivering the supplies to you in their overhead, even while they tell you it's free. And, even for a distributor who deals in more than a variety of supplies, your combined potential order might be too small for the company to want to bother with.

If you're like most publishing entrepreneurs, in the beginning, anyway, you'll probably have to do everything yourself out of economic necessity, from shopping for stationery and office supplies, sweeping the floor, and signing for UPS deliveries. Some local businesses will allow you to set up a house charge account to simplify your bookkeeping, making it unnecessary to dig up some cash and count the change you receive back. Some of these "suppliers" will also offer you a discount for buying in quantity and also for paying before net thirty days.

Even if you do it all yourself, however, it still pays to shop around. When buying office supplies, for instance, you'll probably spend the most at your neighborhood stationery store. The next cheapest source will be a stationery superstore, though sometimes the quality and attention you'll receive is far below what you're used to. In my experience, the cheapest source of office supplies are the mail-order operations that ship the same day your order is received and offer large discounts on volume orders on top of their already low prices.

There are exceptions to everything, however, so the best advice is to take your time and shop around and don't be afraid to dicker. These companies want your business, and if you show you're going to be a good, steady customer, they'll work hard to keep you.

Understanding Taxes

When you first set up your new home-based publishing business and discover how much time, energy, and paperwork you devote to taxes, you might wonder when you'll find the time to work with customers and market your business. Why go into business if most of your revenue will go toward taxes?

First of all, take a deep breath. It only seems overwhelming now as you're learning about your different responsibilities. Once you get used to it, recording and paying taxes—as well as figuring out your deductions—will turn out to consume just a small part of your bookkeeping and office time. As I've mentioned earlier, this is why it's important to keep good records.

You will be required to keep track of your revenue and expenses and to pay a tax to the IRS on any profit your business earns. The amount of tax you pay will depend on the type of business you're running: a sole proprietorship, partnership, or corporation. The tax structures for each differ.

Of course, since the startup costs for most publishing entrepreneurs are pretty high during the first couple of years of business, your expenses may exceed your income, so you won't have to pay tax. The IRS allows that there will be years when you'll earn no profit on paper, even though it assumes you are in business to earn a profit. As a result, many businesses claim a wealth of deductions to avoid showing a profit, and therefore, paying tax. That's why current tax law says that you must show a profit at least three years out of five to prove that you are running a viable business. If you show a loss three or more years out of the five, the IRS may be inclined to audit you. This is why some entrepreneurs, even though they may lose money on paper in a given year, may decide to "forget" about some deductions just to avoid arousing the suspicions of the IRS. Keep in mind that the deductions claimed by home businesses always come under more scrutiny from the IRS.

As for payroll taxes, contact your state employment bureau about the exact deductions you should make for each employee, in addition to the federal tax bureau for information about income tax, Social Security, and other payroll taxes.

Zoning Regulations for Home Businesses

Unfortunately, one of the things you must consider is whether running your publishing business from your home is against the zoning ordinances in your town. Laws can be quite broad when it comes to naming which types of businesses cannot be run from a private home; many of these ordinances were enacted decades ago, when the majority of people working from home were in service businesses that provided a steady stream of traffic into their neighborhood each business day.

Most people just keep quiet about working from home. For many, it's easy, because in most cases, it's impossible to know who's home during the day and who's not, especially in quiet suburban areas.

And even if there is a rule against doing commerce at home, which is how some of the laws phrase it, most people will look the other way if they know a neighbor is working from home and breaking the law. They may even welcome it, because it means that there's someone around who can be alert to suspicious be-havior, or can accept special deliveries for neighbors during the day, although most people have the courtesy to ask you first.

However, there are always those people around who need to stir things up, even if it means that you're not bothering anyone by working at home. If they want to, they can haul you before the town legislators and cite you for breaking the law. And you'll have to prove that you're not. Incidentally, this is how many outdated home-office ordinances are changed, when a home-based entrepreneur who provides tax revenue for the town challenges the laws. Most of the time when this happens in the smaller communities, it makes news, with neighbors lining up for or against.

Whatever the law currently says in your town about working at home, chances are it won't affect you either way. The good news is that as more and more people work at home, the laws will cease to be an issue. The bad news is that there's still a long way to go.

Tax Regulations for Home-Based Publishing Businesses

Once upon a time, home-office tax deductions were plentiful, like back in the 1970s. Working from home—back then, it was usually done in a corner of the sewing room or on part of the dining room table—usually meant taking work home from the office. Either an employee had to bone up and polish an impor-tant presentation the next day or had to meet a deadline.

That corner of the sewing room and portion of the dining room table was typically written off as a business expense. Nowa-days if you were to do that, you might as well draw little red flags all over your tax return, because the IRS is extremely sen-sitized to examine home offices, whether you run your business at home full-time or not.

You can deduct part of your housing expenses if they meet one of three important criteria set down by the IRS to determine whether your home office is indeed a bona fide business expense or if you're just using it occasionally.

- Your home office should be a place where clients, customers, and colleagues meet on a regular basis.
- You should be only using your home office to conduct business, which means you shouldn't be using it as a kids' playroom when you're not there, or as a laundry room. The space has to be used for your business alone. Specifically, the IRS requires that your home office be the principal place of your business—if you're spending less than half your working hours there, you probably can't take the deductions.
- If your home office is located in a separate building, even if you work fewer than three days at home, it's likely that all costs you incur in maintaining that separate building are deductible, including the equipment you use while there.

Of course, there are instances that may diverge from these three criteria. If you're in doubt, you should contact either your accountant or the IRS directly. If you'd like more information, contact the IRS to get a free copy of IRS Publication Number 587: *Business Use of Your Home.*

If you choose to take the deduction, you'll need to fill out a separate form—Form 8829—to attach to your annual tax return. In essence, since auditors are tougher on people who maintain home offices for any purpose, filing this form may lead to an audit. This explains why so many people don't bother to take the deduction at all, even if they qualify.

Because people who work at home in their own small businesses easily pass the test of deducting the cost of the office space, usually the IRS takes less notice. The sticky part comes if you're still working for someone else and receiving a regular salary, since some people who run part-time businesses in addition to working full-time for an outside employer consistently show a loss from the business. You better believe that your return will come under more scrutiny than if you just took the standard deduction from a full-time job, because you'll have to verify your write-offs with figures and logs that showed you actively pursued new customers for your sideline business.

Of course, the best thing to do is to confer with your accountant or other tax professional before you proceed. Examine all the pros and cons before you decide to deduct an expense. And remember: If one area of your tax return catches the eye of an auditor, the rest of your return won't escape notice, either.

13

Technologically Speaking

I hear of many home-based publishing entrepreneurs who start their business with the latest, greatest, and most expensive of everything. Admittedly, it's hard not to be dazzled by top-of-the-line computers, printers, fax machines, copiers, software, and other accoutrements you think you may need in order to start your business. But time and again, I see people with a large credit line and the desire to have the best of everything go totally overboard when it comes to equipping their office. Even if they can afford it, it means they'll have to divert money from the business to make a large interest payment on a credit card or loan.

"I'll grow into it," is how some justify buying a lot of expensive equipment that they don't need. But the danger is that your expenses may be so high from the outset that your business may fail before it even has a chance to "grow into it."

It's entirely possible to equip your office with everything you need for about $2,000. Of course, this assumes that you won't be buying top-of-the-line anything, but rather functional items that serve their purpose and can easily be upgraded—or passed on to an assistant—a year or two later.

In addition, to keep startup costs down, you may decide to rent some of these tools or use an outside service—like a copy shop's fax machine and number—to save money. But I've found in the long run that you're better off buying a fax machine or learning how to lay out and design your promotional materials yourself. Not only will you have more control over your publication, but you'll save time running to the copy shop, dropping off proofs, and waiting to accommodate somebody else's schedule.

Necessary Equipment

Here is a list of the equipment that I find is necessary to launch a business. Even though I make fun of people who I think have gone overboard in purchasing equipment, I'm sure that some will think many of the items on my list are unnecessary extravagance. No matter; this is what I've needed to run my home-based publishing company effectively and efficiently.

Computer

If you're going to do your own graphic design for promotional items, stationery, and other printed materials, as well as laying out copy for your books, newsletters, or other publications, you'll need a computer that can handle graphics programs—like a desktop publishing program. As hardware processors becomes faster and more advanced, the prices will continue to drop. Only a year after I bought my 486/25 MHz computer with a SVGA monitor and 340-megabyte hard drive loaded with software and a fax modem, I found I could buy a computer twice as fast, with extras like a CD-ROM drive, for the same money.

You can skimp on the name brand—not everyone needs the perceived security and value of an IBM. But don't skimp on the machine's capability or storage space (you'll probably have to upgrade them sooner rather than later), especially if you keep all of your business records, correspondence, and designed and typeset manuscripts on the computer. For instance, my old computer had only 4 megabytes of RAM. Since some of the newer programs required 8 megabytes of RAM or more, I upgraded my entire system. Then I got Windows 95, which made my old computer obsolete, as long as there were newer, more powerful desktop publishing systems out there to tantalize me. So I upgraded to a Pentium processor with 90 MHz, 16 megabytes of RAM, and a 1.2-gigabyte hard drive. Even though it was obsolete the day I brought it home, at least now I can use the new versions of QuarkXPress or PageMaker, two of the most powerful and versatile desktop publishing programs.

(If all of these letters and number combinations are like a foreign language to you, start hanging out at your local computer store or ask a salesperson who knows what a computer could do for your business. And start reading the computer magazines—especially *Home Office Computing*. They're filled with tips to help make your computer and your business run more smoothly.)

Some computers have fax modems and voice mail capabilities built into them, but most require that you keep the computer on all the time in order to receive faxes, while others require that you stop what you're working on when a fax comes in and switch to another program. For most entrepreneurs I recommend a stand-alone fax with a dedicated line.

Software

You'll need software to keep track of your finances, write your correspondence and articles, and lay out artwork for ads, promotional materials, and package design—if you choose to do it all yourself. Most people have a personal preference—many times, it's the first word processing program they learned how to use, which means there are a lot of people out there working on software that is painfully obsolete.

Some people swear by Macintosh while others swear at it and prefer their Windows or DOS systems. Ask around and try out a few different programs—many software companies will send free sample disks of their programs so you can try before you buy.

If you're not interested in anything beyond the basics, I'd recommend Microsoft Works for Windows—with word processing, database and spreadsheet programs—and Microsoft Publisher, which provide you with professionally designed templates where all you have to do is plug in the text. For more advanced design, I'd recommend QuarkXPress or PageMaker, both powerful and sophisticated desktop programs.

In the interest of saving time in one area so that I could spend it in another, I bought new software that would computerize my business—QuickBooks, Microsoft Word, and Microsoft Office. I've also bought software so that my computer can handle a new Hewlett-Packard printer and scanner. Beware: When you to see how software can streamline your business life, you may become a bit of a software junkie.

Printer

You could have the best computer and software in the world, but without a decent printer, your printed documents will be mud. Computer printers have gone through as many or even more changes than computers, starting out as dot matrix and daisy wheel printers, then proceeding to inkjet, bubble jet, and laser printers. If you're doing any amount of business correspondence, I feel that nothing less than a laser printer will suffice. Laser printers can handle a larger variety of fonts and can print clearer, crisper letters than all other kinds of printers. Try to get one that prints at least 300 DPI—dots per inch. Better yet, if you can spring for it, go for 600 DPI.

CD-ROM

Try to get a computer with a built-in 4X CD-ROM drive. CDs can hold ten times as much information as a floppy disk—which means software on CD contains a larger number of fonts to choose from than software on disk. In addition, software on CD is usually priced the same—or less—as a program on floppy disk.

Phone with Built-In Answering Machine

I've gone through more than my fair share of answering machines over the years, and I've found that a combination phone and answering machine with redial, mute, flash, and memo features best serves my needs. When I interview people over the phone for books or articles, I can press a button and our conversation is instantly recorded. Of course, an answering machine is optional if you have an answering service or use voice mail features that are offered inexpensively through the phone company. But I prefer to have everything in my office so I don't have to call out to get my messages.

Fax Machine and Phone System

After I bought my fax machine and had it hooked up to its own separate line, I said what anyone who's discovered the benefits of a new piece of technology says: "I don't know how I lived without it for so long."

A fax machine is necessary to conduct business these days, if only because everyone else has them and has become overly reliant on them. And if you want to convey the idea that you're running a serious business, I'd recommend that you have a separate line for your fax machine. Even though I have a business line for my main number, my second line—for my fax machine—can be a residential line, which saves half the cost of a business line.

If you want to reap the revenue that other entrepreneurs do and you do a lot of business over the phone, you must first act like a real business. In my opinion, acting like a real business means that customers calling your number should not be subjected to call-waiting or a busy signal. Also, I feel that serious entrepreneurs should not have a device that tells the caller to press the pound sign to send a fax. Most successful businesses have dedicated fax lines, and so should you.

Voice mail through private systems or your phone company automatically processes all calls that come in while you're on the line. But these systems may not yet be offered in your area.

After many fits and starts, I decided to have call-forwarding put on my line. Now, when someone calls in and I'm on the first line, the call gets forwarded to the fax line, where I've hooked up another answering machine. But even though a fax machine is able to differentiate between an incoming fax call and a call that goes to the answering machine, not all answering machines work with a fax. Mine didn't.

On to the next round. I ordered RingMate from the phone company—a service where one line can have up to four different numbers, each with its own distinctive ring—and I hooked up a device that can send the incoming call to the appropriate machine based on the ring. I still have my dedicated fax line. But when I'm on my first line and another call comes in, it gets forwarded to the first RingMate line, where an answering machine picks it up and the message tells the caller that I'm on the other line. Also, I don't think a plain paper fax is necessary, so until the prices drop considerably, spend your money on something else.

Photocopier

This is not a necessity if you only make a few copies a week. You can rely on the copy function in your fax machine to serve in a pinch when you can't get to the neighborhood copy shop. However, some entrepreneurs who send out lots of regular press mailings say they couldn't live without a copy machine in their office. I couldn't.

Like other electronic business machines, the price of desktop copy machines have dropped drastically in recent years. Be sure to check the newspapers for used copiers; companies that are going out of business will sell top-of-the-line high-capacity machines for a fraction of their new prices.

Other Equipment

You may need additional equipment, based on your personal preferences for a desk, chair, storage units, bookcases, and other pieces of furniture. And if you visit your local chain stationery store, you'll probably see lots of things that you want but can probably do without in the beginning, such as the freestanding label machine, the automatic letter folding and stuffing machine, and the binding device for those specialized workbooks you're thinking of developing in the future. Browse through the store so you know what's out there—it may even give you some ideas for other products and services you could offer your customers. But until your revenue grows significantly, sit tight.

Just remember to go slowly at first, get as much as you need and can afford and then grow with it. You'll know when it's time to upgrade.

Communicating with the Outside World

The office itself and most of our models for information technology to-day are industrial models. The notion of an office really is just a wholesale transposition of industrial processes. We process words in the same way we process metal to put into a car. And when you have a processing mentality, a place for processing, like an office, is essential. But the moment we abandon that processing model and go to stranger and newer models, then the idea of having a physical place where you go and sit down and have a desk and a stapler and all that becomes very quaint.

—Paul Saffo, director at the Institute for the Future in Menlo Park, California

The public's acceptance of what can be done via technology grows by leaps and bounds every year. High-tech companies continue to make George Jetson–like inventions into current reality. And a lot of these new items are making it easier for entrepreneurs to communicate with their clients and outside contractors. At the very least, you'll have everything you need to communicate with the wired world if you have a computer with a modem, an e-mail software package or access to one of the online services (many of the entrepreneurs I need to keep in touch with correspond with me via e-mail), and a second phone line so you can talk on the phone while you're plugged into your computer. A second phone line that is strictly for business—but can be a residential line to save costs—also facilitates bookkeeping and your tax records at the end of the year.

Optional Equipment

If you want to get fancy office equipment, here's what's what.

Local Area Network

If you know you'll need regular access to a client's computer database at any hour of the day or night, you'll need to be equipped with a remote Local Area Network (LAN). Depending on the package, you'll probably be able to access files on the hard drive of your office computer and even print out documents from your client's office laser printer, all from your office.

However, if you need to share files with a client while the two of you discuss it on the phone, or if your client needs to see a document from your hard drive, you'll need to upgrade to document conferencing software, which allows either user to copy a document to a common screen and then send it over the conferencing software and through the LAN network so that both users can view it and make notes on it at the same time. Some programs only allow two people to work together at a time, while others allow three or more users to view a document and make changes.

ISDN

ISDN, or Integrated Services Digital Network, is receiving a lot of attention among wired entrepreneurs in the 1990s. It is the fastest way to send digitalized images over the phone lines. In other words, ISDN will facilitate video-conferencing and the quick transfer of images from one location to another. However, this technology is still being developed, and there's a long way to go before the images are smooth and flawless. In order to get set up with ISDN, you'll need to sign up for a special service with your phone company, as well as purchase hardware that connects you to a LAN, with cameras and microphones on both ends of the line. And that's just the beginning.

Desktop Conferencing Software

Other desktop conferencing programs include several different versions of ProShare by Intel. The basic version allows each person to make notes on the screen, while an advanced version called ProShare Premiere Edition can also tap into a word processing or spreadsheet program that's running on only one participants' computer. That means if you want to do more than just jot notes on a copy of the screen you're both viewing, and actually institute changes to the document itself, these more advanced versions are better suited for you need. Another plus is that even though only one person may have a copy of ProShare, the other can easily download a copy so that the two can work together.

Ideological Differences

What happens when you're working on two different computers, one a PC, and the other a Macintosh? No problem. Another document conferencing system called Face to Face will allow participants to do the same things as other similar systems, even if their computers are not compatible.

The Universal In-Box

What you've probably started to see is the advent of the all-in-one voice mail, fax, speakerphone, and e-mail, all in your computer. One wit has already referred to it as the "universal in-box." Indeed, it does make working from home easier, especially if you're short on space. Voice-recognition software will also make this system as hands-free as you like. All this technology means you'll soon be able run a business by yourself with no trouble at all.

Cellular Everything

Some devotees of the virtual office are already touting cellular and wireless faxes, e-mail, and downloading capabilities (even though their performance often leaves something to be desired). Again, as with other high-technological devices, the glory of these truly magical instruments of communication is still unfolding, while the bugs are being ironed out, which include lots of static and unexpected disconnects, usually at the most inopportune moments. With cellular modems it seems the faster the transmission speed, the more likely mistakes will be made. In addition, data signals sent via cellular lines can be easily eavesdropped by anyone interested in your words. And encryption software for cellular data is still under development.

But when the bugs are finally eliminated, you will be able to run your business out of a cabin in the middle of the woods— or somewhere on a beach. As long as Federal Express and UPS still deliver everywhere, you'll be able to run your business wherever you want, if that's your dream.

The Big Boy

Even AT&T is getting into the act. In early 1995, the company began taking out full-page ads in the *Wall Street Journal* and other newspapers and magazines, touting their new computer system called The Globalyst 360 TPC. The headline: "Introducing the first PC&C for work-at-home. It's a speakerphone, a fast modem. It's listening to voice mail while you're sending a fax. It's how to eat the Big Boy's lunch." It certainly is marketed to those comfortable running their own business, calling their own shots while the guys in the suits and ties forty stories up are fighting unproductive power struggles and jockeying for promotions.

Further down in the ad, AT&T tells how they designed the Globalyst: "We listened to what people like you said about how they work. And created a solution that works like an entire office. Complete with secretary."

Maybe not quite that, but it also boasts a separate combination speaker and microphone that's not built in to the computer; a good thing, since with a conference call you might want to relax on your sofa and not be confined to your desk. The system also contains a built-in personal phone directory that works with caller ID to match a number or a name, so you know whether it's a client calling or the long-distance phone sales rep trying to get you to switch your service.

The Alternatives

Of course, you could just use a typewriter, or a paper and pencil, to conduct business. And if you're on a tight budget, this may be all you're able to do.

Some people decide to buy used computer equipment, especially if they are unable to rely on technical support staff. Hard drives crash and programs freeze up—of course when you're on deadline—and if you have a client who is less than tolerant of the marvels of the computer age, you might run into trouble.

If you can't buy new equipment, try to get a used computer system or other office equipment with a warranty. I've found that buying used computer equipment from an independent service tech who regularly installs corporate systems and buys back their old systems will give you your best value, especially if they provide a warranty and allow you to call in with problems, even if all you have is a stupid question.

Protecting Your Investments

One thing you should definitely do is buy a surge protector for your computer, fax, copy machine, and other electronic equipment. Electrical power supplies are often unpredictable no matter where you live, and the power can suddenly spike, that is, suddenly increase. Without a surge protector to absorb that excess power, the surge of electricity can enter your electrical equipment, which may fry all the inner components and render them useless.

Besides a surge protector, you'll also want to be sure that you don't have your office located in a room that is the point of entry for your electrical service. Again, excess surges are a factor, and they can quickly fry your computer to a crisp, although you wouldn't notice it until you try to turn it on and nothing happens.

Moving Data—and Other Stuff—Around

One problem you may encounter is the need to transport documents, equipment, or samples back and forth between your office and clients' offices.

In recent years, more and more entrepreneurs are using their cars as a part-time office base, whether it's intentional or not. A professional resource group in Boston, the Yankee Group, reports that currently six million Americans work from their cars most of the time, and millions more use their automobiles as a temporary base at least some of the time. Both of these figures will increase by 25 percent in the next five years, says the Yankee Group. The bad news is that most of these vehicles—more than 90 percent—also double as the family vehicle. So if you've just dropped your daughter off at day care and she left her lunch box or toys on the back seat, and you're about to pick up a major client at the airport in fifteen minutes, you're going to have trouble.

To solve this problem, or at least to make the vehicle look as corporate as possible from the outside, some people rely on tinted windows. Others have a vinyl sheet or blanket they use to just throw over any offending materials that have been inadvertently left in the back seat. And still other people may relegate any junk to a trunk that locks.

There are special organizers for the car that can be secured to upholstery or carpet with Velcro, which not only keeps it from sliding around but can also be moved in an instant when a corporate dignitary is seen approaching your car without warning. And still others may choose to rely on a conversion van, where the back is living and/or working space, with a divider between the back and the front. Some people even totally convert their vans to a mobile workspace in the back, complete with computer, fax, printer, and files. And, of course, a cellular phone.

Getting Technical Help

Because you'll be working for yourself, one problem that you may run into is the lack of a technical support team. That's why it's good to have an agreement with a freelance technical whiz who you can call when trouble comes up or when you don't feel like waiting on hold for an hour with the manufacturer's technical support group.

Also, software that troubleshoots computer problems can make your life a bit easier. A program called WinSleuth Gold provides you with a detailed analysis of what's going on with your hardware. Another good program is called System Info Plus, a shareware program that provides an analysis of your hardware system, in addition to performing a number of tests to further help winnow down the possible list of problems.

If you need help occasionally with your high-tech equipment, or if something isn't doing what you want it to do, some office-supply companies and computer manufacturers will provide technical assistance to individuals. Often, you'll have to sign up in advance and provide proof of purchase, and sometimes a fee is incurred, but you can't beat this kind of personalized assistance, especially when you don't want to jeopardize the relationships you have with your clients.

When Space Is Tight

If you need a break from your home office but still have a deadline to meet, a laptop computer works wonders: You can use it to work in the living room, the bedroom, or even outdoors, if you feel like it. Another advantage is that laptops don't take up a lot of room, an important consideration if your office is tiny.

Because of space considerations, you may need to consolidate other pieces of your office equipment as well. Now you can buy a machine that combines a phone, answering machine, fax, copy machine, and printer, all in one.

High-Tech Furniture

If you've been in any of the chain stationery supply stores, you've undoubtedly seen their all-in-one desk consoles and workstations, which are probably better than anything you've worked at before. Before you buy furniture impulsively, carefully consider what you need and how you're going to work. Do you need a desk that fits into a compact space, or several tables where you can spread out papers, books, and other research materials?

One major manufacturer is gearing up to concentrate at least one of its furniture lines specifically toward the home office worker. In 1994, Crate & Barrel, the nationwide furniture and houseware retail chain, introduced a new line of furniture that's designed to accommodate the needs of small business owners who work from a home office. Some pieces feature table wings that easily fold out of sight when you're through working, as well as a built-in document holder that tilts to the angle that's most comfortable for you. Crate & Barrel will also create a complete home office furniture system, complete with desk, bookcases, and drawers. Each piece of furniture is designed to deal with the wormlike tangles of power cords usually found in a home office, which can be a problem if your foot accidentally dislodges the power cord to the tape recorder during an interview. The new furniture at Crate & Barrel is designed to prevent these types of mishaps.

However, don't expect the same low prices you find at Staples and other warehouse office-supply stores. Each piece of this new furniture is made of solid cherry—not particle board—and a simple writing desk will be priced at $599. A complete office set up will go for about $2,500. With the success of Crate & Barrel's marketing drive, the warehouse stores can't be far behind, with lower prices to boot. At the same time that Crate & Barrel was introducing its home office furniture line, the warehouse chain Office Depot was planning to bring out their line of home office furniture.

Who knows? Soon, home-based entrepreneurs may be able to shop at a store called "Home Office Depot."

A Temporary High-Tech Office

Kinko's copy centers, the national chain, is quickly earning a reputation among entrepreneurs as a bona fide business partner who will bend over backwards to help your business succeed. Kinko's is not only open twenty-four hours a day in most locations, but they can provide copies, fax machines, computer rentals, and telephone ports. They're also making it possible for entrepreneurs to conduct video-conferencing sessions from their centers. Some even offer the use of private conference rooms for business owners who need a base outside of their home. In fact, Kinko's is promoting its centers with these capabilities as a virtual branch office for entrepreneurs who need to perch there once in awhile.

And AT&T is perfecting its version of the picturephone, which was inspired by a device in *The Jetsons* cartoon series. Unlike the earlier crude models, this new style of picturephone can deliver and receive clear, full-motion images across standard telephone lines for no additional cost. However, the model needs some additional work before it is introduced to the public, which should happen sooner than was expected simply because demand is so strong.

Setting Up Your Office

When you're working for a large company and you feel physically uncomfortable in your cubicle or workspace, usually the only choice you have is to just grin and bear it. Thankfully, things are more flexible in your home office, where you can design your work space according to your work habits and temperament.

If you're working from home, it's important that your work space be in a separate room, if possible. Not only will this suffice for tax purposes if you decide to deduct the cost of a home office from your taxes, but it will also send a message to both yourself and your family and friends: "This is a work space, and when I'm in there and the door is closed, it means I'm busy working." Conversely, it also means that you can close the door when the workday is over, and you can shift gears into your personal life. One thing about working at home: It's very hard to ignore your work when it's always near. That's one of the few advantages of working in a regular office: You usually stop working when you leave the office. It's important that you set up the same arrangement at home.

I've always worked from home, and though I've had a separate room for an office several times, most often I set up my desk and computer in a spare alcove with no door. Not only does it make it hard to leave it behind at any hour of the day or night, but books, papers, and other work materials have the uncanny ability to overflow into other areas of the house. If I want to eat at the kitchen table, I usually have to transfer piles of papers, books, and bills to the sofa, and then when I wanted to sit on the sofa, well, you get the idea.

So get a separate office!

It's also important that the space you choose for your home office be free of distractions. If you have room on the quiet side of the house, set up your office there. And if there's a television in the room, get it out! You don't want to have even the tiniest temptation to wonder what Luke and Laura are doing when the clock reads 3:13, so the best thing to do is to remove the TV from the room before you ever begin to work there.

Future Technology

Future technology to be utilized by entrepreneurs will incorporate cellular networks so that you can use phones, faxes, and computers without being plugged into a wall jack. Another innovative technological development on the horizon involves portable phone numbers, which automatically follow you by punching a few buttons on your phone. And as entrepreneurs begin to assume more of the responsibility for doing what expensive secretaries used to handle, the handheld computers called personal digital assistants (PDA) will become more prominent in the home-based publishing entrepreneur's world.

As complex fiber-optic cables are wired across the United States and overseas, the ability to communicate by both voice and image will certainly be enhanced. For instance, the fiber-optic cables in use in 1994 can process 25,000 calls at once. As these cables become more sensitive and are put into service along heavily used telecommunication routes, they will be able to process 25 million calls at once, or the equivalent of 25,000 television signals.

The experts like to say that as small businesses become more popular and the communication technology becomes more highly developed, our business world will get used to the fact that information commutes, not people. Besides high-service fiber-optic cable, one truly space-age high-tech development involves the assigning of private telephone stations to an individual in much the same way as a telephone number is assigned to you today. A system called the Bidirectional Unicable Switching System, also known as BUSS, will make it possible to have exclusive video-conferencing no matter where you go. Each person using BUSS will subscribe to a cable system and receive the equivalent of a TV station signal. Though this technology is still in development, it will someday be commonplace.

Employment analysts believe that the quick development of interactive technological systems like BUSS will help the United States stay competitive in the international business world.

14

Finding Money for Your Home-Based Publishing Business

Finances, ugh. Why can't I just run my business and be content that the financial end will take care of itself? Because if all you do is deposit checks and credit card orders and write checks to pay your bills, you may never know if you're earning a profit or not. If you don't keep track of the financials, your publishing business can quickly stumble, and then go down the tubes altogether without your ever knowing the reason why.

It's not too difficult to keep a handle on the various financial aspects of running your business. If you take some time early on to set up the finances for your business, you'll probably end up spending much less time on it down the road.

Profits and Losses

One important way to gauge how your home-based business is doing is to calculate a profit and loss statement. Even though business revenue may be coming in regularly, it is quite possible that you are actually losing money because your expenses exceed your income.

Keeping accurate records is the first important step in creating a profit and loss statement; then all you have to do is plug in the numbers. There are two kinds of profit and loss statements: one that projects your estimated profits and losses, and another that keeps track on a weekly or monthly basis to show you how your business is doing. You can also compare the two, and if your projections are either 20 percent higher or lower than your actual figures, based on slow and peak times, you can adjust your projected profit and loss statements as you go along.

Here's how it works. First, calculate the revenues you expect to generate each week, month, and/or year. Say your average sale is $54, and you project that you'll make 300 sales in your first year. The total estimated gross revenue is $16,200. At this point, carefully review the numbers, adjusting them upward and downward to see how your revenues would change with an increase and decrease in business. In addition, you should consider all the work that is necessary to generate 300 sales of your product: I'll tell you now that it's a lot harder than it looks.

When you first start out, your home-based publishing business probably won't be a huge moneymaker for you; but wait, you haven't even gotten to your expenses yet. Get out the list of estimated operating costs you drew up in Chapter 12 (see page 108), and add up all of your expenses for the year. You'll include postage, printing costs, phone bills, rent and utilities—*everything*.

Don't forget about depreciation. Ask your accountant for advice on this, but chances are that you'll be able to deduct a certain amount each year for depreciation on your house, office equipment, and other big-ticket items. This is not strictly an expense, but it will lower your profit, which will then lower your tax bill.

And don't forget about the interest you pay on any loans connected with the business. Also remember that the type of business you run—sole proprietorship, partnership, or corporation—will affect your profit and loss statement.

After deducting all of your expenses from your revenue, you'll be left with a pretax profit or loss. There's one more step, though. Now deduct all of the taxes you pay in connection with your business—except payroll taxes, which are figured into your payroll expenses—and you will come up with your actual net profit or loss, which probably seems a long way from your initial gross revenue figure.

Though you'll always have certain fixed expenses, there are a variety of ways you can adjust your profit and loss statement: cutting your expenses, discounting or raising the price you charge for your products and services (which I don't recommend), or increasing your marketing efforts, to name just a few. Over time, you will be able to see what attracts new customers and what keeps old customers coming back. You'll also see that running a business is a continuous experiment; your profit and loss statement is merely a reminder of how well your experiment is going.

Keeping Track of Your Money

Most home-based publishing entrepreneurs use a variety of methods to help them keep track of their money, both revenues and expenses.

The basic record will probably be your checkbook. There are a number of business checking accounts with built-in ledgers that allow you to record your expenses under different categories at the same time you write a check. Separating these expenses in advance makes it easy at the end of the year to determine how much you've spent in each category, and if you need to cut back in an area.

Some entrepreneurs prefer to keep their financial records on computer. Software now exists to enable you to track your expenses, categorize them, add them up in a flash, and even write checks printed on your computer printer.

To keep track of revenues, create a record for each customer, what they purchased from you and how much they paid, how they heard about you, and whether they bought anything else from you in the past. There are a number of specialized software programs which help you track revenues and expenses, and provide other features such as word processing and database tracking.

Whatever method you choose, make sure it's easy to use and that you check in with it at least once a week. Going longer than that will make keeping track of your money a chore and something you're likely to put off, which will more likely lead to mistakes.

Fortunately, some of the companies you'll do business with are making it easier for their customers to keep track of their money. Credit and charge card companies now offer a breakdown of charges in different categories on their monthly statement. Some of the suppliers with which you maintain an account will also provide this service. And if they don't already do this, ask. They might start.

Developing Your Credit

If you're in business for any length of time, you're going to need credit in one form or another. Most of the time, it will be your regular suppliers who won't accept cash or checks with each delivery. Not only is it too unwieldy and increases the possibility of loss, it's a big waste of time.

But most suppliers and other companies won't offer you credit unless you've done business with them before. It's the age-old catch-22—how can you develop your credit if no one will give you any in the first place?

Fortunately, there are ways around this. Many companies will open a credit line for you based on your personal credit record. They'll usually start you out small, and then increase your credit line as your history with them grows. Needless to say, you'll help your credit line if you always pay promptly, even before the due date—and by acting promptly whenever they or you have questions about your account.

With other suppliers, you'll need to prove yourself in the beginning, and your personal credit, no matter how stellar, will have nothing to do with it. These companies will make you pay cash or by check *before* they deliver the goods, and only after a certain period of time will they begin to extend you credit, and only a little at a time at first.

After establishing a good credit record for your business, you'll undoubtedly be solicited by charge card companies to open a business account with a high credit limit and low monthly payments. Though having business credit card accounts help in many instances—such as renting a car or buying airline tickets—try not to use them too much. Credit cards are almost universally accepted today—even the IRS takes MasterCard and Visa now! Because it's easier to slap down the plastic than to apply for a basic account with a supplier, you might be tempted to run up huge bills at high interest rates. But there is a price to pay for this apparent convenience. Instead, use them sparingly, appreciate them for what they are—an extremely expensive way to borrow money—and be as judicious as you are with your personal creditors. Or rely on American Express, where you have to pay off your balance every month.

Although banks can be a lot choosier now about lending money to people with even unblemished credit histories, you might apply for a line of credit at your bank, that is, if you haven't already done so. Learn to rely on it only in emergency financial situations, and pay back the money immediately. A line of credit will help your business get through the tough times, and you *will* have them.

How to Finance Your Home-Based Publishing Business and Still Have a Personal Life

Where are you going to get the money to support yourself and your family while you're getting your business up and running? And where are you going to get the money to invest in the business?

It's next to impossible to plan your new business without talking about how you're going to finance it. But it's usually not the lack of money that prevents most people from taking the first step toward becoming a home-based publishing entrepreneur. Instead, the fear of losing a familiar structure to one's life is what stops most people dead in their tracks. But most people don't want to admit to this, so they use finances as an excuse.

Many people use a combination of savings and current income from a job to finance their new business. Others take out personal loans or max out their credit cards to pay for their startup. Some people will take in a roommate or rent out their houses or a few rooms to cover their expenses, and I've heard of other people who pare their living expenses way down and subsist on Kraft macaroni and cheese dinners until the business starts pulling in a few dollars. However you do it is for you to decide. If you've already mapped out the reasons why you want to start your own home-based publishing business, and have begun to plan what you have to do next, then you're ready to tackle the financial part, which is probably easier than you think.

Obviously, if you're single with no dependents, you're going to have an easier time getting your financial house together so that you can start a home-based business. If you're in a relationship and/or have kids, it may be a bit more difficult in the beginning to juggle time with your family and friends, not to mention keeping everybody fed—including yourself—while you start to get your business off the ground. But many publishing entrepreneurs have told me that if it wasn't for their personal cheering sections, they may never have succeeded at their businesses.

Another way that people finance all or part of their businesses is by increasing their work hours before they leave their jobs, or by taking a temporary part-time job once they launch their businesses.

Should You Go into Debt?

Though many start their own home-based publishing businesses using a combination of savings and pared-down living expenses, some do not hesitate to go into debt. Still, it makes some people—and me!—queasy to think about borrowing a lot of money in order to finance your own business.

One advantage of taking on debt to finance your business, of course, is that you can eliminate your money worries in the beginning, when you most need to concentrate on launching your business and making a good impression, which will allow you to better focus on what you want to accomplish. The major disadvantage is that you have to pay the money back, with the first payment usually due a month after you first receive the loan. Sometimes, the pressure of having yet another bill when you're trying to cut back on your personal expenses can be enough to distract you from your main purpose for starting a business: breaking away from the pack and heading toward financial independence.

Here are some questions to ask yourself before you borrow money to finance your business. Write your answers in your notebook. If you're considering going into debt, it's a good idea to ask yourself the following questions *before* you fill out the loan application:

- What's the least amount of money you think you'll need to borrow? Can you cut it down even more?
- How much time will you need to pay it back? How will the loan be repaid?
- How do you plan to borrow the money—by personal loan, a second mortgage or home equity loan, credit cards, your credit union, or from a friend or relative?
- Can you delay the first payment until after your business has started to generate revenue?

Of course, if it doesn't bother you to go into debt, go right ahead. But being a business owner can make you so independent that you won't want to rely on anybody else, especially when it involves money.

How Much of a Monetary Risk Are You Willing to Take?

When you start your own home-based publishing business, it's very likely that you'll have to get used to a drastically lower income, at least in the beginning.

In your notebook, answer the following questions before you quit your job to start a business:

- How much money have you budgeted to live on during the launch of your business, and afterwards?
- Do you think of yourself as a risk taker?
- If you had to suddenly get used to living at a level one-third to one-half of what you're used to, could you do it if it meant you were working for yourself?
- With your loss of salary and job title comes a loss of status. Do you see it as a threat if you don't have a job that you and others can identify with?
- What will your immediate family think? Will your decision to accept a lower salary put a crimp in any of their plans?

Borrowing Money

The issue of borrowing money in these credit-weary days is apt to be a sticky one among entrepreneurs who may need to take out a loan to finance their business. "I'm in enough debt already," you may say, "Why would I want to borrow any more?"

Sometimes your cash flow won't keep up with your expenses. Even if you and/or a partner holds down a steady job, trust me when I say there will be times when even that won't be enough. Operating a home-based publishing business with all of the expenses that continue steadily from month to month will eat up huge amounts of cash, and during those times, it may be necessary to borrow money.

If you have a rich relative or a sizable trust fund, you can skip over this section. But if you're like most of us, you'll need to rely on a conventional financing source. And since you already know to anticipate these cycles, especially if your business is known for its sharp peaks and valleys throughout the year, you should take steps beforehand to line up an available source of credit for the times you absolutely need it.

I know of many entrepreneurs who have drawn on their credit cards to initially finance their business, and then have gone back to them again when things got slow. At anywhere from a 12 to 21 percent annual rate of interest, this is definitely an expensive way to borrow money. Even if you fully intend to pay it back before interest has a chance to accumulate, there will be times when you are only able to make the minimum payment.

Some entrepreneurs form partnerships solely for this reason: to have a silent partner with deep pockets who's looking for a good rate of return. But if you prefer to have a partner for other reasons—or to go it alone—and you don't want to rely on your credit cards, there is another option, and that is to open a line of credit at your bank.

If you don't want to go this route—or get turned down for it—there is the old-fashioned way, and that is to save for a rainy day. When business is booming and revenue is strong, set aside a certain percentage—some say 20 percent of every check that comes in—and sock it away in an interest-bearing savings account. Don't invest your funds in a place where you can't access them instantly; even though the interest rate may be less, you'll probably lose money paying a penalty for early withdrawal from an IRA, mutual fund, or other investment. A money market fund is best; the interest rates tends to be a little higher than a passbook savings account, and you have immediate access to your money.

How to Raise Additional Capital

Because the revenue from your business will be sporadic at times, many publishing entrepreneurs turn to other sources of income.

If you need to raise additional capital to finance your business, you may want to turn to parents or relatives. Others rely on the proceeds from the sale of their primary house, and move to an area where they can live mortgage-free so as to plow all the revenue from the business back into the business.

You have to be creative to stay in business these days, regardless of your venture.

How to Give Credit to Customers

The primary way that most entrepreneurs extend credit to their customers is by accepting the credit cards that are popularly used today. MasterCard, Visa, American Express, and Discover are accepted by many small businesses. The credit companies will charge a fee to set you up with their service, and then you'll pay the credit company a percentage of every transaction made by a customer, usually 2 to 5 percent. Your account is typically credited within one to three days after you entered the transactions into the system, and there are certain restrictions each company places on its members, depending on the amount your business will gross each year, among other factors. It is relatively simple to apply for privileges to accept credit cards from your patrons, although you may have to jump through a few hoops with financial statements, tax returns, checking account statements, and other proof that you run a trustworthy business.

It may seem unfair, but credit card companies prefer to grant merchant status to retail businesses with an actual storefront because customers actually see the total amount on the slip they are signing. Mail-order businesses are immediately suspect because they're not dealing with the physical card. It's easy for unscrupulous businesses to take advantage of the system, to debit hundreds of thousands of dollars from accounts, wait until the money is deposited to their account, and then disappear. Don't laugh—this was the explanation I was given when I was turned down for merchant credit card status.

Fortunately, my bank (the one place I had been warned would be almost impossible to receive credit card merchant status from) ended up accepting my business, based on a personal recommendation from my bank manager, who was familiar with the amount of money flowing in and out of my business account. The transactions in that business account helped establish that my business was here to stay; plus, I had been banking with them for six years.

My advice is to keep applying for credit until you are accepted, because your revenues will instantly increase once you are able to accept credit cards. If you decide against it, you may never know how profitable you may have become. Indeed, whether or not you accept credit cards may be the difference between business success and business failure. It's unfortunate, but true. Before I started taking credit cards, one man sent me his credit card number with instructions to start his subscription. I wrote back and told him we weren't set up to accept plastic yet, and to send a check. I never heard from him again.

Here's a hint: If you get turned down by a credit card processor who handles MasterCard and Visa, call American Express about getting merchant status from them. American Express isn't as picky and stringent in the requirements it places on small businesses, and once you develop a track record with American Express, the other companies will be more likely to accept your business.

However, some entrepreneurs ultimately decide not to accept charge cards from their customers. Either their volume is too low to justify paying the commissions, or else the credit company places too many restrictions on them. Some have also said that the companies tend to have a patronizing attitude towards smaller companies because they simply don't generate the commission revenue that larger businesses do.

Other entrepreneurs believe that if customers really want to do business with them, they'll find a way to pay, whether it's with a credit card or a check. But as I've already said, many products and services these days are often impulse buys, and credit cards make it easy for your business to capitalize on your customers' impulses.

Any way that you decide to extend credit to customers, it's important that you do offer it in some form. We have a love-hate relationship with credit in our society today, but since we do rely on it, you should arrange for it before you start your business, if at all possible.

Improving Cash Flow

Even though the cash flow in your business will be highly erratic at times, you can, to some extent, predict when your cash flow will slow down and when it will pick up. This will help you figure out which months you should stockpile excess cash for the times when cash flow and income are way down.

Cash flow is defined as the pattern of movement of cash in and out of a business: revenue and expenses. If you apply for a loan with a bank or other financial company after your business is up and running, you'll have to provide an analysis of your cash flow; if you're just starting out, you may be required to provide the loan officer with a projected cash flow statement.

Cash flow includes all actual monies coming in and going out of the business, and includes cash, checks, and income from credit cards. Depreciation of your computer and other office equipment does not factor into your cash flow analysis.

The first step to improving your cash flow is to increase your business year-round. But the effects from this aren't always that immediate. There are things you can do to even out your cash flow. You might consider special promotions designed to pull in more business during those slow times of the year. For instance, you should plan to mail promotional offers to past customers in your slow months. Or you can send out direct mail packages offering your new products and services to past and present customers as well as those who have never purchased anything from you, but have inquired about your business in the past.

Another way to even out your expenses and therefore improve your cash flow is to ask your utility companies to average out your payments so that you basically pay the same amount each month year-round.

15

Day In, Day Out

When it comes time to utilize the vast array of resources available to help you start your home-based publishing business, one of the best ways to begin is to dive headfirst into it all. In this chapter, I discuss the many experts, resources, and groups you can draw on to help make your business as strong as it can be.

Your Own Advisory Board

Whenever I start a new publication or a new project, I think about my own experiences and how they relate to what I would like to do. I consider how I plan to market these products, and reflect on marketing techniques that have worked well for me in the past as well as the problems I faced, whether I solved them or not.

But I also draw on the experience of others in the field. For example, when I decided to start a newsletter to help small travel businesses market themselves better, I called up innkeepers and travel outfitters that I had talked with over the years when I wrote travel articles for magazines and newspapers. I asked them about their marketing problems, what they'd like to see more information on, and other topics. Their answers helped me to refine my focus and allowed me to add a number of article ideas to my file as well.

Though many, but not all, businesses have an advisory board, I decided to form one for my newsletter *Travel Marketing Bulletin*. The purpose of my advisory board was to add credibility to my business as well as gather a group of experts whom I could call upon for advice and suggestions. When I assembled my advisory board, I looked for a cross-section of small travel business owners, most of whom had some specific expertise in marketing. I selected three persons: an innkeeper who had gotten her inn written up in most of the top magazines, the owner of a large western travel clearinghouse who booked tourists on everything from dude ranch vacations to llama-packing trips, and a woman who served as communications director for a small California winery whose aim was to attract tourists to the winery tours.

I provide all of the members of my advisory board with a free subscription to the publication. Every few months I call each of them up to ask what they think of the business, and to solicit new story ideas. They also provide me with the latest news from their respective industries. Sometimes I would publish their information in the newsletter; other times, I would just file it away.

Some large businesses with advisory boards pay their members a stipend in exchange for meeting once a year, usually during an annual trade conference that the majority of people in the business attend. I don't think this is entirely necessary, especially when you're first starting out. As long as you let your advisory board members promote the fact that they're important enough to have been selected for the board, and use their membership on the board as a way to further their own careers, it's usually enough for them. A big reason why I have an advisory board, however, is that it gives my business a stamp of approval whenever I include their names, companies, and reputations in my promotional materials. Even though the person who receives my direct mail letter may not have heard of any of the members of my board, just having an advisory board is usually enough to impress.

Finding Writers for Your Publishing Company

Sooner or later, many home-based publishers discover that they prefer not to do all of the writing for their businesses themselves. Indeed, some know this at the very beginning, and arrange to have some or all of the articles written by outside contributors, or by an editor who works for you in-house or on a freelance basis. How do you go about finding writers in the first place?

Look for experts in your field who will consider a byline in one of your publications as a credit to their reputation and expertise. For instance, with a cookbook for working mothers, you could ask around your area for the names of nutritionists and dietitians who work with busy working mothers—but it doesn't even need to get that specific. Any nutritionist with a decent background and a desire to provide specific information—and willingness to help market the publication—would be a good bet. Or you could call local, state, and national professional organizations for some referrals.

Another good place to start is at your bookstore. Ask them for the names of authors who have written on the subject you want to cover in your new publication, and who may want to expand their reputations. The advantage here is that they already have written materials that can be easily edited and adapted to the format of your publication.

When you contact the various professional organizations, also ask if you can place a notice in their association newsletter to alert members that you're looking for writers. You may be flooded with inquiries. But I'd caution you against soliciting writers through writer's organizations and magazines. It's been my experience that you'll receive many submissions that are totally inappropriate for your needs.

Trade Associations

As is often said, it's not *what* you know, it's *who* you know. And membership in a variety of business associations can help you start your business and foster its growth. Joining a trade association can be invaluable in the beginning because of the contacts you can make as well as the advice you'll receive from people who have been running a business in your industry for a long time. Membership is increasing in many professional industry organizations and business trade associations, so you'll have access to many more experts and mentors to call on for advice.

In addition, organizations that focus on a variety of specific issues that you'll deal with in your business—whether it's computers, producing specialty foods, or owning a retail store—exist both on a national and regional basis, with state chapters of the large organizations as well as individual specialty groups. For example, I belong to the Vermont/New Hampshire Direct Marketing Association, a group of professionals in my region who both focus and dabble in direct marketing. We meet every four weeks for a luncheon, talks, discussion, and networking. I've found that these meetings bring to light the issues that are frequently discussed in business magazines.

I recommend that you join an association that covers your industry as well as apply for membership in one of the more general publishing trade associations. Most associations publish a regular newsletter for their members, sell literature that covers specific aspects of your industry, and hold occasional conventions where members can network with each other, attend workshops, and visit trade show exhibitors who sell products that are pertinent to the field. Some associations also offer their members consultation services at reduced rates, credit card acceptance privileges through a clearinghouse, health insurance, and long-distance and toll-free number services at a discount. Though yearly membership rates can be high—sometimes up to $200 a year or even more—most entrepreneurs report that it's worth it for all the benefits, networking, and ideas they receive to help them enhance their businesses.

In addition to the national trade associations, there are many regional, statewide, and local organizations that home-based publishing entrepreneurs can also join. These usually benefit small business owners by providing local marketing opportunities as well as a reliable source of feedback. For instance, some of the smaller associations are started by a group of local members of a particular national organization. They meet through the national association, talk regularly on their own, then decide to form their own chapter. And some entrepreneurs even start their own associations for their trade.

Consultants

Almost as quickly as new businesses have been popping up all over the country, there has been a bevy of consultants to help novice entrepreneurs, as well as established business owners, work on some of the problems that occur when a business grows. These consultants help fledgling entrepreneurs learn about running a business by speaking at conventions, seminars, or one-on-one meetings. In many cases, these consultants have also written extensively in their field, drawing on plenty of first-hand experience to steer their clients in the best direction. Some consultants will also hook you up with a business in which you can work as an intern to see if the field is right for you.

New seminars and conventions for aspiring and experienced entrepreneurs are scheduled all over the country on a regular basis. The best way to find one in your area is to check the notices and advertisements in the home-based newsletters and magazines published by your national and regional business and communications associations, as well as by independent publications for the trade.

Training Courses

Many of the trade associations and convention organizers who specialize in your industry also hold special workshops solely for entrepreneurs who are just getting started in their fields. And I've also seen community colleges, adult education schools, and even computer centers offer a wide variety of business courses on their regular schedule. Even though some of the topics covered in these seminars may not entirely apply to you and your business, it's still a good idea to attend all the classes; you may get a new few ideas.

To find out about these courses and be alerted to upcoming workshops and seminars, write to the organizers and ask to be placed on their mailing list. Most courses that don't take place within a community school format will last a few intensive days, and will provide you with a condensed bird's-eye view of the business. Some involve strictly sit-down classroom learning, while others may require you to create a business plan over the course of a few days. This kind of workshop usually begins on a Friday and doesn't let up until the participants collapse Sunday afternoon.

Magazines and Trade Journals

Many of the business and trade associations that cover your industry publish specialized magazines or home-based newsletters on topics that concern their members, as well as provide insight into how recently passed legislation and tax information will affect the industry in the future. There are independent journals as well. Write to the industry-specific trade associations to find out about them.

The Small Business Administration

The Small Business Administration (SBA), financed by your tax dollars, is a veritable gold mine of information for those wanting to start their own business. There are three major divisions within the Small Business Administration that can assist you in the startup phase of your business, as well as provide advice and assistance once your business is up and running.

One division is the Small Business Development Center (SBDC), which counsels entrepreneurs in every conceivable type of business and at every level of development. The SBDC will set you up in private sessions with entrepreneurs who have experience in your field. You can ask them about any phase of your business, from marketing to financing, or how to keep the business afloat during tough times.

The SBA also runs the Small Business Institute (SBI) on a number of college campuses nationwide. Each SBI tends to specialize in a given field, from engineering to business management, but if you're looking for very specific information, contact your nearest SBI. The assistance at an SBI is largely provided by students in the program, but always under the watchful eye of a professor or administrator.

The Service Corps of Retired Executives (SCORE) can be another exciting place for you to get information about your business. SCORE officers provide one-on-one counseling with retired businesspeople who volunteer their time to help new entrepreneurs like you. Each volunteer counselor has extensive experience in a particular field, and is eager to share his or her insights. SCORE also offers a variety of seminars and workshops on all aspects of business ownership for aspiring business publishers; you'll also get specific advice about the nuts and bolts of running a business, from bookkeeping to taxes.

The Small Business Administration also has a program to loan money to small businesses, but you have to apply through a bank. The SBA then kicks in some of the funds and serves to guarantee your loan based on your business plan. The SBA also offers a large variety of helpful booklets and brochures on all aspects of running a business.

To locate the SBA and its other programs, look in the white pages of the phone book under United States Government. Call the office nearest you for information about local programs and services.

To directly contact the SBA in Washington, write to them at:

The Small Business Administration
409 Third Street SW
Washington, D.C. 20416

To get in touch with the variety of services, call these numbers for immediate help:

SBA Answer Desk: 800-827-5722
Or go online with the SBA at 800-697-4636

Tracking Your Progress

In some cases, it may be pretty difficult to know in advance how quickly you'll progress in your business, and how it will happen. But if you draw up a plan in advance and can check your progress against your business plan every week or month, you'll have a guide to follow and tinker with as you proceed.

Hint: If you're like me and tend to drastically underestimate the amount of time it takes to accomplish a certain task, do yourself a favor and overestimate the length of a project.

Getting—and Staying—Professional

Sometimes it may be difficult to maintain a professional image while you're working at home—maybe in comfortable clothes, and perhaps even in your pajamas. This is one reason why many entrepreneurs choose to stick to a regular schedule and even get dressed up when they're working at home. Here are some suggestions you can implement to build that image of professionalism in your home office.

Maintain a separate phone line for business calls. Have one line and restrict its use to your office only—don't run extension phones off of it into other areas of the house. And only *you* should answer the phone. Don't have your kids answer the phone, even if you're off in another corner of the house for a minute—don't even have your partner answer it. The phone should only be used for business purposes.

Take charge and let your independence motivate you to be in the office at a set time each day and accomplish what you set out to do. People who work at home not only tend to work more hours than their office counterparts, but they also are usually able to work for several hours at a stretch without interruptions, which would be impossible in most office settings. One of the biggest benefits of having your own business is that you can work during those times of the day or night when you are most productive. For instance, if you're a night owl, you're free to work into the wee hours. Or if your mind is clearest first thing in the morning, then you can jump right in at dawn.

This may not be a possibility for every home-based publishing entrepreneur, but frequently you can schedule individual projects for those times of the day when you're at your best.

Should You Get Dressed Up for Work?

Some people look forward to working at home because they can spend the day in their pajamas and don't have to waste valuable time each morning just to look presentable. Just think of the time you'll save!

Unfortunately, there are an awful lot of people out there who will think that working in their pajamas is akin to lolling around the house on a lazy Saturday afternoon. Their productivity will suffer because of it. In that case, you just may have to fool yourself that you're going to the office, even though your commute may not be no more than ten steps from the bedroom to home office. Indeed, there are a number of people who just don't dress up as much as they would if they were going into the office for the day.

Animals in Your Home Office

You may not have considered the issue of having a cat or dog hang out with you while you work, but if you are a pet owner, believe me, the issue will come up.

Perhaps you'll deal with it simply. Maybe the cat has already thrown up once on the printer, or the dog tried to jump up on your lap and in the effort knocked your coffee into the computer keyboard. So from simple experience, you'll close the door to keep out not only your kids and neighbors, but also your pets.

For the rest of you, however, it'll be a little different. Picture this scenario: You're stuck at home working, and if you don't have employees, you still feel a bit lonely. You don't want human company, but a living breathing *something* in the room might be nice, especially if it does nothing more than just sleep.

I've always had my six cats work by my side when I'm sitting at the computer or sitting on the sofa writing. It helps me keep up with my rhythm, and they're usually content not to require your full attention if you're not paying attention to another human. Which means when you're on the phone, they might cause trouble, like walking on the keyboard before you've had a chance to save that important report you've worked on all morning, or even stepping on the phone to disconnect you. Of course, these are all accidents, but they do happen from time to time. Still, I spend a lot of my time working by myself, whether I'm talking on the phone or not, and I do find that cats are the perfect companions to get me into the groove of working.

Of course, there are drawbacks. When I bring my computer to be serviced once a year, my computer technician always asks if a mouse has been living in the computer (he always pulls out big clumps of gray fur from around the hard drive). Cats and dogs can be insistent, and sometimes when I sit on the sofa and talk on the cordless phone and one of my cats is nearby, she will not hesitate to let me know by vocalizing that she is unhappy that I have stopped petting her. Customers usually ask if I have a baby, but I say, no, it's a cat. Although some people may find this explanation to be awkward if you're trying to convey a professional image, one unexpected benefit is that something like this usually helps to break the ice.

Taking a Break

When you work in an office, even though you may not take an official coffee break, typically your entire workday is punctuated by regular interruptions—by coworkers, phone calls, running errands, going to meetings. These interruptions help break up your work and keep you from working too long on one thing, so they're both a good and bad thing—the breaks help to keep your mind fresh, but they can also prevent you from getting all your work done.

The lack of breaks for most people working from home largely accounts for the increased productivity of many entrepreneurs. However, you need occasional breaks in your day to relax your focus and give you a chance to recharge. One way to take a break is to vary the kinds of work you do each day. Write for an hour or two, then make a few phone calls before reading over a couple of new pertinent journal articles that just came out that week.

Another important way to take a break is by getting away from your work, whether it's going to the kitchen for a cup of tea or going for a walk. Even fifteen minutes will do it. And if you don't need to be by the phones constantly, you may even want to take a long lunch hour and eat at the local coffee shop, then pick up a few groceries or the dry cleaning on the way back.

Some people also take a break by exercising. Granted, it's easier to exercise regularly when you're working from home than on the days when you're in the office because you probably won't have to fight locker-room gridlock and the post-aerobic traffic jam in the shower. If your schedule is flexible, take your lunch early or later in order to avoid the workout crowds. However, many entrepreneurs say that even a quick walk around the block is enough for them to clear their heads or give them some perspective on a particular problem that had been bothering them.

No matter what your reasons are for taking a break, the important thing is to do it. If you don't, you may burn out on your work, which you probably don't want.

Balancing Your Home and Work Life

When it comes to the topic of working in the same place that you live, you'll probably get one of two reactions from your friends:

"That sounds great" or

"Ugh, that would be awful."

Rarely do you find a person who is neutral about the topic of working at home. Sometimes, however, a negative reaction is due to lack of living space: a studio apartment already crammed to the hilt will leave little room for a home office.

For other people, however, the problem lies in the belief that home is for the personal side of life; they have no desire to let business permeate their domestic walls. Some people will not be convinced that it's actually possible to successfully mix work and home under one roof. For everyone else who is interested in the concept but needs a little guidance in how to mesh the two successfully, here's some help.

The first thing you need to do is to make sure that there is a distinct line between your home office and your living space. If this isn't possible, for instance, if your at-home work space is relegated to the dining room table, then you should try to gather your work into a box or closet at the end of each workday, and especially on the weekends.

Then, you need to set small goals and rewards for yourself. For instance, promise yourself that when you finish working on a report, you'll take a walk around the block. Things like that are necessary to balance your home and work life so that your living space doesn't just turn into a work space.

Half-Time Analysis

After you've been running your own home-based publishing business for awhile, usually after a couple of months when you've had some time to reflect, it's a good idea to evaluate your overall experience—consider the areas in which you've met or exceeded your goals, as well as areas in which you need improvement.

The purpose? To see what is working and what isn't. It gives you a chance to adjust your work style, or to decide if you want to continue working in this vein for the foreseeable future. A close analysis at this stage will point up areas where you fall short, and allows you to concentrate on the parts that you enjoy most and do best.

So be honest and answer the following questions in your notebook (in as much detail as you want):

- Do you feel that you've accomplished the main goals that you set out to do? How so?
- List the five most important things you've learned about your work and yourself as a result of running your own business, and tell how you learned them.
- List the five things you didn't learn but wanted to. How would you change your day-to-day operations to place more priority on them?
- What do you want to do differently from now on, if anything? What do you want to remain the same?
- What are you going to do now with what you've learned?

What If You Feel Isolated?

One of the most common complaints of entrepreneurs in making the adjustment to their new lives is the loss of face-to-face contact with other people. Here are seven ways to help relieve your feelings of isolation:

1. Get in touch with other entrepreneurs, whether they're in the publishing business or not. Also check to see who else in your neighborhood is working from home. Though I can tell you in advance that most other home-based workers won't take kindly to being interrupted during the day for a *Kaffeeklatsch,* you might want to make an informal contact and then offer to have both of you keep your options open. For instance, you could offer to accept express mail packages on the days when he or she is called out of town, and this person may ask you for tips on the best way to get a contract from your company. Don't push it, however, especially if you sense

that a particular person is not crazy about the idea of socializing during the workday (or after) with a stranger. For this reason, I think your best shot is to socialize with other entrepreneurs in your field.

2. Take a break by going online. Both CompuServe and America Online have "working from home" forums where you can find solutions to your problems of isolation or even give some advice to others who are going through what you've already dealt with. Sometimes, these Dear Abby sessions can even materialize into fruitful working relationships.

3. One advantage of being an entrepreneur is that you're not required to be in your home office for every minute from 9 to 5. This means that you don't have to save up all your aggravating errands—like running to the dry cleaners or taking your dog to the vet—for Saturday when it seems like everyone in the neighborhood has the same thing in mind. You can also look to these errands as a way to beat your feelings of isolation. Once you visit the supermarket or dry cleaner during the day for a few weeks in a row, perhaps the people who work there will chat with you.

4. If you regularly took an exercise class or participated in some activity when you worked in an office, then try to do the same thing when you're working from home. This may be a good case for involving other home-based entrepreneurs in your neighborhood. Find someone and go for a walk or a swim at lunchtime.

5. Set up a network of other entrepreneurs in your industry for an e-mail round-robin. Someone poses a question or problem, and everyone in the round-robin gets to offer their two cents on the subject. After awhile, there are no questions asked, just an ongoing series of advice and comments. Members of this group could live hundreds or even thousands of miles away from each other, it really doesn't matter.

6. Call your local chamber of commerce and find out if they have a group of members who are home-based entrepreneurs and who meet regularly.
7. Establish a regular schedule, and then stick to it. Nothing causes the feeling of isolation more than if all you do is work. People who live by themselves are especially prone to this. Unless you have regular overtime, when five o'clock arrives, try as hard as you can to leave the office and close the door. Then get out of the house and hang out where there are other people around.

Troubleshooting

It's a hard thing to admit that the extensive business plan that you pondered, planned, and worked on for so long somehow isn't working out. Should you keep plodding on and hope that it gets better? Or should you scrap your plans entirely?

Of course, you should realize that, as I mentioned earlier, working from home may be very different from what you expect. So if what you're doing doesn't feel quite right, ask yourself if your initial expectations for your business were too high. Most of us have had a project we worked on that didn't live up to our expectations. If that's the case, try to figure out what went wrong, write it off, and try again.

If you're running your own business, however, you really don't have much time to waste figuring out what's wrong. After all, you're supposed to be working. If your work falls off because you're trying to figure out another approach to being an entrepreneur, your clients may decide that you're not committed and take their business elsewhere.

The first thing you have to do is determine where things have gone awry. Ask yourself the following questions:

- Did you over- or underschedule your time?
- Did you expect too much from your business?
- Are you still adjusting to working from home?

- Or did you start your own business based not on your own desires, but somebody else's? Or what you *thought* you wanted, and not what would truly work for you?
- Are you working all the time?

If any of your answers to these questions indicate that you need to revamp your daily routine, then make some changes. Sometimes, people who run their own businesses get so excited about their ventures that they actually can't stop working.

Being a publishing entrepreneur requires you to take a broader look at yourself, and recognize both your strengths and shortcomings. If you've been running your own business for the wrong reasons, you might just have to scrap your entire plan and return to a regular job, even though you may not like it.

So if you're having trouble, it's especially important to quickly evaluate what's gone wrong so you can retool. Concentrate on why you feel that being an entrepreneur is definitely worth it, think about the reasons why you decided to start your own home-based publishing business to begin with. Rededicate yourself to your business, change your focus, or take a few days off to gain some perspective. But don't let your discontent remain unaddressed for too long, or else it will begin to affect your business.

16

Marketing

Marketing is a term that can make a good number of home-based publishers uncomfortable. Nevertheless, it is one aspect of publishing that they need to know and use effectively to survive in the business.

Close your eyes and think: What does marketing mean to you? Most people would think advertising, and not much else. It's no wonder you envision expensive, glossy ad campaigns on TV and in national magazines; or you may feel that there's either something mystical about the ability to draw in customers on the strength of just words and/or pictures.

You don't need a degree in marketing to sell your product effectively. In fact, you'll able to sell it better than a professional because you know your business best. Also, you're probably not doing what everyone else is doing who's earned an expensive degree in marketing. Sometimes marketing people tend to view marketing with almost a herd mentality: Innovative thinking, in terms of completely new ideas for an ad or publicity campaign, is usually frowned upon simply because it's *too* different. Translation: "How do you know it works?" If you're thinking of hiring somebody to do your marketing, forget about it. *You* are the best person to promote your business. After all the time and money you'll spend on starting your home-based publishing company, you will probably regard it as your baby. Who better than you can convey your love for your products?

Marketing can actually be fun— just think of it as one of your most creative tasks. In fact, the more creative you are, the more business you'll be able to pull in. As the owner of a home-based publishing business, you have two big advantages over the big guys: speed and innovation. Marketing ideas at big corporations have to be sliced and diced by hundreds of people before they see the light of day. By that time, they have usually become so bland as to be ineffective for attracting attention. Needless to say, this process also takes an inordinate amount of time.

But you can market your business differently. You're small enough to be able to come up with an idea and to have it in place the same day. You can be outrageous or refined, depending on your mood and what you want to accomplish.

The Purpose of Marketing

Unless you let people know you have a great product, you won't be able to attract even one customer. Last I heard, ESP is not generally recognized as an effective marketing technique.

"Oh, they'll find out about me somehow," you'll reply. But *how* are they going to hear about your publications in the first place? More importantly, how are you going to convince them to buy your book or newsletter once they *do* find out about you? With *marketing*.

And how are you going to locate the kinds of people who will be most interested in your publications? Through *marketing*.

"My brochure knocks 'em dead," you say. But how are you going to get it in the hands of potential customers in the first place? It's great if your brochure and other promotional materials really convey what readers can expect if they purchase one of your publications or other products. However, you must first let them know that you exist before they can send you a check.

The purpose of marketing is to develop and execute a number of different strategies that target prospective customers; you want to inform them about one of your publications or your company, and then convince them to give you a try.

Always keep in mind that marketing in whatever form will help you to attract new customers, and also will help to keep them purchasing from you year after year. The best thing about loyal customers is that you incur very little additional marketing costs to secure their patronage. They're already familiar with the merits of your publications and the integrity of your company, and you don't have to spend time or money trying to convince them of it.

Defining Your Market

Americans are largely overwhelmed by media messages today, and some research has shown that most people don't pay attention to the majority of the ads they see. But the messages they *do* notice are the ads that reach out to a specific interest of theirs. And if an organization they belong to recommends a certain product—your book, software program, or other publication— you can bet they're going to listen and respond.

Remember that you won't be able to reach everybody who would benefit from your publications, and even if you could, your message is only one of thousands they see and hear every day. The first step to reaching your customers is to target your ideal customer.

Defining your ideal customer means that you can then narrow down your choices of how to reach them, as well as the best methods to use. Ask yourself the following questions:

- Who is the most likely type of person to buy your product? Then describe two *other* groups of people who would also benefit from your publications.
- What magazines and newspapers do they read? What TV shows and radio programs do they prefer, if any?
- Which organizations do you think they belong to?
- Does their physical location play a role in whether they'd be more likely to buy from your company? For example, does it matter if they live in a city, the suburbs, or a rural area?

- What is their income range?
- Why will they decide to buy from your company ?
- What do you think would make them decide *not* to buy?
- What do you think their goals are for five, ten, and twenty years in the future? How will your home-based publishing business help them to reach their goals?

Writing Your Marketing Plan

Without a concrete plan to follow, it's easy to let marketing fall to the bottom of your daily and weekly to-do lists, or even forget about it entirely. One way to make marketing your business tolerable and sometimes even enjoyable is to map out a specific plan for each month and year that won't let you off the hook so easily.

Like having a business plan, it's important that you develop some kind of marketing plan so you'll have a blueprint to follow in the months ahead, as well as a way to evaluate what has worked for you in the past, as well as what hasn't.

When drawing up your marketing plan, make sure that you have enough lead time for the special events and promotions that you're planning. For instance, it's never too early to think about Christmas as far as national magazines are concerned. In fact, the best time to send a press kit to a national magazine about your annual activities is in July.

Developing a marketing plan can be a simple task—like writing up the goals you'd like to achieve in the next six to twelve months, or a more complicated one—like determining market and revenue projections as well as the percentage of the market you'd like to grab from your competitors.

In your marketing plan you'll need to define your purpose as well as the target audience you wish to reach with your marketing arsenal. You'll also need to design a marketing budget that is reasonable but aggressive, and pick your choice of media, along with the methods you'll use to evaluate their results. This will help you adjust your marketing plan for the following year.

Developing a marketing plan for your home-based publishing business will provide a long-range perspective to spread your efforts among a variety of opportunities. It will also help you to anticipate certain events that happen once a year. But the plan is also meant to be tinkered with. For example, perhaps a specific advertising issue comes up in September, or you hear about an idea that has worked wonders for another similar business nearby and you want to try it. You look and see you don't have much marketing scheduled for November and December; it may be worth it to take the money from those two months to pay for the project in September.

There are four different aspects to a marketing plan: The amount of time you will spend, on both a daily and weekly basis; the type of marketing you plan to do, from concentrating on magazine publicity, newspaper ads, or revamping your brochure and business cards; the amount of money you want to budget for each month and for the total year; and who's going to carry out each task—for some businesses, only one person will be responsible for writing copy, working with a graphic artist, and doing interviews with the press. Even the smallest home-based publishing businesses may decide to farm out the responsibilities to ensure they get done and to provide a fresh eye. The type of customer you'd like to attract also enters into each of these aspects, broken down by region, profession, gender, income, and interests.

To draw up your annual marketing plan, you'll have to cover a lot of areas. You'll need to be as detailed as possible to design the best marketing plan for your business, and to incorporate a little bit from each of the following:

Advertising: Buying ads in radio, newspaper, TV, magazines, and other media.

Direct Mail: Sending brochures and sales offers to prospective and past customers, writing and editing a promotional newsletter.

Publicity: Sending letters, press releases and kits, and making follow-up calls to media contacts. Write-ups can consist of a full feature or a brief mention of your company in a roundup, or service piece.

Other areas: Planning special events, trade shows, working with the chamber of commerce and other businesses on cooperative ventures, for example.

In your notebook, write down your answers to the following questions. Again, be as specific as you can.

Time:

- How much time do you think you will need to spend each week on marketing?
- Provide a breakdown of how many hours you'll spend each week on publicity, advertising, direct mail, and other areas. Do you feel this is enough time? Do you think you are planning your time effectively?
- Would you like to spend more or less time? What would you spend it on, or where would you cut back?
- When do you project your busiest time of the year to be? How far in advance should you begin planning marketing projects so as to capitalize on this time of year?

Media:

- In which medium would you like to focus the majority of your marketing efforts?
- What type of marketing brings you the most customers?
- What kind of customers would you like to win over? How would you reach them?

Budget:

- What percentage of total sales does your marketing budget comprise? How could you increase—or decrease—that amount? What other categories could you take money from?

- Would you like to invest more money in one or more categories? Which ones? Why?

Execution:

- Name the person or people who will be responsible for marketing. Is there anyone else you feel comfortable assigning additional duties?
- Are there additional tasks you could assign to a staff member that you don't like to do or don't have enough time for?

Customers:

- In which area of the country do most of your customers live?
- Are your customers concentrated in one industry, or are their professions not a consideration to the services you offer?

Think about your answers to these questions for a few days. Is there anything missing?

Finding Prospects

You probably have a good idea of the type of person who is likely to become your long-term customer. Now, how do you go about finding that person?

There are numerous ways. You should know, however, that prospects are not the same thing as customers. What I'm about to say may take the longest to sink in of anything else I present in this book: Even though your publishing business is your baby and everyone tells you that it's great and that they'd buy your products in a minute, the fact is that *only a small percentage* of people who write or call for information about your company will actually become customers—and it might take awhile for them to decide to do so. You must view every prospect as a potential customer, and treat her or him with the same respect as if they were one of your paying customers, but you shouldn't be disappointed or surprised when they don't buy.

Think of how many offers you're exposed to each day, or about the sheer number of products that you walk by every time you go to the supermarket. Of course, you only end up buying and trying a fraction of what's out there, and unfortunately, most of your prospects will regard your product as just one of many. That is why it's absolutely vital that you spell out exactly how they'll benefit by buying one of your publications. We have become a society of fishermen: Because there is so much to choose from, we feel we must know all there is to know before we make a decision. And even then, there's a little voice in the back of our heads saying, "There's always something better."

Marketing is not always advertising, as many people wrongly assume. In fact, advertising is one of the least effective and most expensive ways to find your prospects.

Think about your target customers and then figure out how you can reach them; use some of my suggestions as a jumping-off point. You'll undoubtedly be able to think of many more.

Cloning and Keeping Good Customers

Once you get a good customer, hold on tight. And don't let go. The good news is, like that shampoo commercial where one person tells two friends and so on down the line, your good customer knows other people who could also turn out to be good customers. After all, word of mouth is probably the most effective kind of marketing there is.

There are a variety of ways you can "clone" good customers. One way is to ask your current customers if they know of other people who would like to receive information about your company and products. You can include a separate form in your mailings to ask each customer or potential customer for names, including space where they can fill in the names and addresses of friends. Then you can keep track of any orders that you receive through this referral system, because if a friend becomes a customer, you can offer the first customer a discount on future purchases, a technique that will also boost your response rate.

I know of one home-based publisher who sends a discount coupon for 10 percent off a future workshop sponsored by the company to current customers and encloses an identical coupon for the customer to give to a friend. Treating your repeat customers to discounts each time they purchase from you is, in essence, a kind of "cloning," because they are likely to come back again and again.

The best way to keep your repeat customers coming back is to continue to market to your targeted group of customers, and by maintaining the quality of your products and your customer service. After all, one of the reasons why customers reorder from you is because they know what to expect. In other words, there will be no surprises.

Finding the Time

Finding the time to market your home-based publishing company and its publications is one of the biggest problems that you'll face. I spend 90 percent of my time on marketing and only 10 percent on writing. Even when I'm under deadline, I still try to do some marketing work every day. You should, too. The next time you say you don't have time to market your home-based business, consider these tips:

- Because you need to figure out which marketing techniques are bringing in the most customers, it's important to ask each customer or potential customer how she or he heard about your business or about your products. This information should then be tabulated to determine your rate of return on paid advertising and where you should plan to spend more of your marketing in the future. Seeing the exact number of dollars that you have pulled in from each of the previous year's advertisements, promotions, and direct mailings will make your media-buying decisions much easier. And it also becomes much easier to say *no* to pesky ad salesmen whose publications don't work for you.

- A lot of marketing involves grunt work: stuffing envelopes, making lists, shuffling through ad rate cards. Do this during slow times of the day or night; it's easier to justify when ten other things aren't demanding your attention.

- Examine your slow times, whether it's every Monday or the month of March. Set up the following year's strategies by writing your marketing plan, and then perform maintenance tasks on your weekly slow day.

- Hire someone to carry out your plan if you truly can't find enough time, or give the responsibility to a staff member. One home-based publisher hired a PR consultant who was just starting out. She paid the consultant a below-market rate, but tied bonuses into any increased business that resulted from the additional publicity. Some home-based publishers say that novices are better than experts; although they don't have the contacts, they also don't have a lot of preconceived notions about what's right and what's wrong. With marketing, it's innovation that gets attention.

Advertising on a Budget

Advertising is a type of marketing where you pay for a certain amount of space or time to present your message to a particular kind of audience. Since you're paying to send the message, you can say anything you want—time or space and money are the only factors that limit you.

But consider the limitations. Advertising doesn't really give you much leeway. In fact, because you bought the space, you're obviously selling something, and most people turn right off when someone's trying to sell them something.

The primary mistake that many new publishing entrepreneurs make in their marketing is to rely too heavily on advertising, both when they're first starting out and later on as well. I'm not saying that advertising doesn't work, because in some cases it can pull quite well. However, it often turns out to be the most expensive way to reach customers, especially when your one-inch display ad is only one of hundreds in a particular publication.

Advertising is easy, and also a known entity with a tangible product—but it doesn't necessarily produce results, that is, an increase in the number of customers. Advertising is attractive because somebody else does all the work: you tell the sales rep what you want to say, you write out a check, go over the proof, and receive a copy of the magazine. Spending your time and money on promotion—whether it's sending out a press kit or renting a booth at a trade show—is harder, and doesn't provide you with a guaranteed entity, i.e., an ad in print, but what it will do is provide you with increased exposure among your targeted customers; they'll notice you simply because you'll stand out. The majority of businesses take the easy way out, spending the bulk of their annual marketing budget on advertising and perhaps printing another 1,000 copies of their brochure with what's left over.

Take a look at the ads in your local newspapers and magazines. What do they look like? How do they make you feel? Is there one in the entire publication that makes you want to drop what you're doing, pick up the phone and call? Probably not. Do the same thing the next time you're watching TV or listening to the radio. Pay close attention to the locally produced ads. Again, do they make you feel excited about whatever it is the advertiser is trying to sell? Again, probably not.

The vast majority of advertising in all media is placed to gain consumer awareness, to let people know that a business exists. And this type of advertising can build business for your products—but very slowly. By the time you're able to notice any results from your advertising program, you may already be out of business. It's also difficult to measure. How often do you go into a store and say that you heard their radio commercial? Unless the owner is a friend of yours, probably never.

Because advertising is so expensive, you can't waste money to use it just to let people know you're there. Publicity and other more direct marketing tools exist for this reason, and they're also cheaper.

The only reason you should spend money to advertise is to back up a special promotion or discount that's available for a limited time, or to offer customers a chance to respond to your ad and receive something for their efforts. A toll-free number, a discount coupon, or a special incentive will help you measure how many people responded to your ad. Then you can see if the ad paid for itself, and whether you should pay for another one in the future.

Some home-based publishers report that they sometimes feel pressure from a newspaper or magazine editor to advertise in exchange for a promise to cover their business in an editorial section of the publication. Though most editors will deny it, I can tell you that it *does* happen. However, this form of coercion is most likely to occur at smaller publications, where most or all of their revenue comes from advertising. And when the publisher also serves as the editor, you can be sure that any conflict of interest between advertising and editorial departments will frequently be ignored.

If you do decide to advertise, don't settle for the quoted rate. Always ask, "Is that the best you can do?" Especially if the publication is nearing its closing date and there's still ad space left to fill, the sales rep or ad director might let it go at a significant discount. In addition, radio and TV stations and publications frequently offer a special rate to first-time advertisers in the hopes that they'll become regular advertisers. At other times, they'll offer a discount if you advertise in a special section or sponsor a certain program. Again, you should always ask for discounts.

Radio and TV advertising doesn't usually work effectively for home-based publishers since their primary audience is far too specific for this broad form of marketing. It's best to focus on print ads in the publications that you know your target audience reads. For instance, some of the publications in which I advertised *Sticks* included single-state lifestyle magazines, which focus on regions where lots of readers want to live, but don't. And so *Vermont Magazine, Vermont Life, Montana Magazine*, and a small newsletter called *Vermont Property Owners Report* had brought good results for me.

If you're interested in advertising in a particular publication, call the advertising department and ask for a media kit. You'll probably receive a fat folder with a copy of the magazine, a rate card, and lots of material that shows the demographics of the magazine's readers, comparing the numbers to other similar magazines. Sift through them and take out an ad on a one- or three-time basis in the beginning. Contrary to popular belief and to what ad sales reps say, if an ad doesn't pull for you after a couple of times, your response rate sure isn't going to improve after the seventh insertion. So give it a shot if you think it might work and pull it before you start to lose a significant amount of money.

Marketing on the Internet

Since 1995, use of the Internet as a business marketing tool has increased rapidly; for small businesspeople, there's almost no way to ignore it as an economical way to gain exposure for your business. A lot of attention has been paid to the potential of the Internet as a way to make money. But amidst all of the information, one thing is certain: You can't just create a Web page and wait for the orders to pour in. Many potential customers will visit your site for initial research about your company, and then call your 800 number for a print catalog and place an order by writing a check and sending it via "snail" mail. At this stage of the game, the Internet mainly offers novelty and represents yet another way for people to collect information.

Many big businesses pour thousands of dollars into the development of their Web sites, and then get most of their satisfaction from the perception that they're a technologically hip company. As a small company, you can't afford to be this complacent. The good news is that by combining traditional marketing methods with some high-tech wrinkles, your Web page can do more than stand as a bits-and-bytes version of your print marketing materials.

Before you spend all that time and money to establish a presence on the World Wide Web, be clear about your intentions. Many businesses have jumped onto the Web either because they sell pots of instant gold or felt they had to do it because everybody else was doing it. So carefully consider your reasons for going online and whether it will be worth it, at least in the near future.

Beware of companies that sell advertising space on the Web or other Internet sites and inform you that your ad will be able to reach thirty million people. I don't know of any site that generates that much traffic, and besides, that audience is usually spending a lot less time at any one site than they would with another form of media. You're better off spending the money to develop your own Web site.

Though many businesses are rushing headlong into establishing Web pages, if you're just getting your feet wet in cyberspace, start small with just an e-mail address through one of the online services. You can then expand your own presence by advertising in an established electronic shopping mall or until you become familiar with some of the nuances and subtleties of using the Internet.

Publicity

In the opinion of many home-based publishers—myself included—publicity is the best kind of marketing you can buy. That's because aside from the initial costs of preparing a press release and contacting the media about your new publication, publicity is free. When a writer reviews one of your publications in a magazine or newspaper, or when a reporter spotlights your company on radio or TV, it is considered by many to be an endorsement of your business. Audiences naturally respond more favorably to an unsolicited endorsement than to a paid ad.

An insider aside: Editors, writers, and reporters at media large and small will rarely review a publication that they don't care for. First off, they don't have the space, and they don't want to waste their own or their audience's time. So, in most cases, if you see a publication reviewed in a major magazine, it's likely that the editor and/or writer has weeded out less useful publications in order to give more space to the one that was chosen.

Just as you must pinpoint your ideal customer, you must also narrow down your choices of media. Your ideal customer will often select your media for you. For instance, your target customer is probably interested in other subjects related to that in your new book or publication; he or she is probably reading publications on related topics. So what you need to do is contact those same publications in the hopes that an editor or writer will want to tell their readers about you. However, if your topic is *too* close, the publication may consider you to be a competitor and permanently freeze you out.

First, look at the masthead of a publication to get the name of the editor who usually handles the topic related to your publication, or the writer whose byline regularly appears on stories about your topic. Never contact the editor-in-chief of a large and/or frequent publication—that person will be far too busy to respond to you. The managing editor or an associate editor is a much better choice.

For instance, if you want to publish a cookbook for working mothers and you're looking for customers, you could send a press kit to all of the women's and parenting magazines, as well as to the food magazines and newspaper editors who handle these subjects. You can also rent mailing lists for these subscribers and then send a direct mail piece their way. Or maybe you could go to a busy supermarket, stand at the exit, and hand out sample recipes and a brochure to exhausted-looking women with children in tow. Better yet, if you're good at making a presentation and at public speaking, maybe you can work out a deal with the supermarket to hold an in-store demonstration using foods the manager wants to push and those that fit in with your menus and recipes. Then the store might include a blurb about your appearance in its weekly advertisements and you could do your own promotion the week before by appearing on local TV and radio talk shows and arrange to be interviewed by your local daily and weekly newspapers. You'll also want to arrange to have a reporter cover your demonstration so that the next time you schedule an event, people will know to come, or contact the reporter before the event.

There are literally thousands of ways to promote your business and products, but I think you get the idea. But before you do any promotion, you'll need a press kit.

Anatomy of a Press Kit

There are many aspects to marketing that scare people off—for some it may be the queasiness of selling yourself, for others, the perceived expense—but perhaps one of the most intimidating is the notion of putting together a press kit. Common reactions range from "I don't have thousands of dollars to invest in some fancy press kit" to "What goes in it?"

In short, this is what goes into a press kit:

- Cover letter
- Press release
- Copy of your brochure and other promotional materials
- Bio sheet—in other words, some information about *you*
- Press clippings
- Glossy black-and-white photo
- And a folder to put them all in

Why should you have a press kit? To make it easier for a writer or producer to do a story—or even help them make the decision to do a story about your publication in the first place. Writers and radio and TV show producers often need more information than can be found in a brochure. And for print stories, they'll need a photo that's easily reproduced, which isn't usually possible by reprinting a picture from your brochure.

More importantly, however, a press kit provides this information in a language that media people understand. Even though you may find the format and tone of the material in a press kit to be overly commercial and self-congratulatory, it throws the emphasis on you and/or your publication and presents the facts—the cake, so to speak—so a writer can concentrate on getting the personal details—the frosting—when the time comes to interview you over the phone, which tends to pass more quickly than either of you would like.

Here's a brief rundown of the contents of your press kit:

Cover Letter

This should be brief, usually no more than one page. The first paragraph should consist of one sentence, and that line should be enticing enough to quickly draw the reader in. I frequently like to word it in the form of a question. In the next paragraph, answer the question you posed, and then tell how your publication will help the editor's readers improve their lives in some way, whether it's to save time or help them to relax. Then tell why you're writing to the editor at this particular time, whether it is to alert the media to a special event or to provide them with an introduction and background material on your publication.

Then provide a few story suggestions that fall into that particular media's genre and that don't wholly focus on you.

Press Release

This should cover the five W's of newswriting—who, what, where, when, and why—again with an enticing lead followed by brief paragraphs that are to the point and provide the media with background information. Mention should also be made of the timeliness of whatever you're writing about.

Bio Sheet

Essentially, a bio sheet is your resume in prose format. Sometimes an editor or producer will decide to do a story on your company or publication based on your own personal history, so it helps if you play up something about your life that is unusual or follows current trends in your story. In fact, start right off the bat by making it your headline. For instance, if you've always dreamed of helping people to design their own home gardens and have finally written and published a book on the subject, then say so, and say it early on.

Press Clippings

Journalists are well known for their herd mentality—often they won't cover a story unless somebody else has done it first. But contrary to popular belief, it's *not* difficult to get press attention—in many cases, all you have to do is ask for it. If you're new in town, you have a new publication out, or if you've done something new at your company, that's news and you should contact a reporter about it even if you haven't been written up in the past. Try it; you'll see how easy it is. Contact the business editor at your local daily or the features editor at your local community weekly paper.

Glossy Black-and-White Photo

Though a newspaper will frequently send a photographer to take a picture to accompany a story about you and your publication, some of the smaller papers don't have the budget or the time, and they'll usually publish whatever you send them. A 5-by-7 or 8-by-10 glossy black-and-white photograph—usually a picture of the front of you sitting at your computer taken at a slight angle—will do. Don't send color prints or slides unless they're specifically requested. You may want to enclose another picture—perhaps a full front shot showing you holding a copy of your book or publication—but it's not necessary.

A Folder to Put Them All In

Nothing fancy here, just a plain folder with pockets you can stash all of the above in neatly. Some home-based publishers put a label on the front that lists the name of their new publication along with the name of their publishing company, their town, state, and phone number, but the label isn't essential.

On occasion, a reporter or producer will ask for individual pieces from your press kit. This is typical, so don't be offended that she or he doesn't want to see your entire masterpiece.

Think of your press kit in this way: It's a capsule of your business or publication designed to make a member of the media interested enough in you and your business to want to tell readers or listeners about you. And this, of course, is the best kind of advertising you can get.

Direct Mail

Most people refer to direct mail marketing as simply "junk mail." But as American life becomes increasingly busy and complex, people are more likely to respond to an offer they receive in the mail, whether it's for a well-earned vacation or a case of dog food.

The secret to effective direct mail selling is to first select a mailing list that will "pull," in direct-marketing parlance, and then to tinker with your sales letter, order form, even the color of the envelope until you find the combination that brings in the best response. Entrepreneurs who use direct mail for even a small percentage of their marketing will discover that it can be compared to a game of golf: They know they can always score higher, so they never stop obsessing over it. In the case of direct mail, however, a little obsession is a good thing.

A direct mail piece needs to be carefully crafted, because most people don't respond to an unsolicited offer unless the literature clearly answers all of their questions.

There are hundreds of books that will tell you how to write and design an effective direct mail package, but at the very least, here's what you'll need:

- Letter: It can range from one to four pages, or even more. Experts say the longer the letter, the higher your response will be. Remember that your readers must feel comfortable sending money or a credit card number to a company they've never dealt with before.
- Order form: Make it easy for people to respond. Look at other order forms or the subscription cards you find in many magazines. Then make sure that it fits in an envelope.
- Reply envelope: I usually use a #9 envelope with my return address printed on it so that customers can easily slip in the card. Some publishers arrange to pay for the postage, but this can become expensive. I've found that people don't object to using their own stamp, but some mail order experts assert that it cuts down on the response.
- An envelope to put it all in: I put my return address in the upper left-hand corner with a teaser of some kind in the lower left. This brief phrase should entice the recipient to open it up, which is sometimes a great challenge, especially if you send your package bulk rate.

With these four pieces, you'll have a bare-bones direct mail package. If you can add a sheet that provides even more information about your publications—perhaps on colored paper—again, your response rate should increase.

Trade Shows

Trade shows and expos are a great way to get your business before the eyes of a large number of people who are willing to buy . . . or to help them decide what to buy in the future. Though preparing an exhibit at a show requires a lot of time, planning, and money, on a per-prospect basis, a trade show is one of the best ways to meet potential clients, as well as touch base with existing customers.

If you're thinking about exhibiting at a trade show, visit one first to get an idea of the other exhibitors and of how you could do with a booth. Ask the other exhibitors if they come back to the show year after year—a good sign if they do—and check out the booth layout to see where you'd like to have your booth next year. At some trade shows you can get away with a low-tech homemade look, but this approach may work against you at a trade show where most exhibitors have costly, high-tech displays. Then, before you send in your deposit for a booth at a trade show, call a few of the exhibitors—with businesses both similar and different from yours—from the previous year's show and ask how they did there.

Working with Current Customers

You've probably heard it said that entrepreneurs get 80 percent of their business from 20 percent of their customers. There is a lot of truth to this statement, although a lot rides on how one treats current customers.

Often the best marketing technique to use with current customers—and future ones as well—is to *simply smile*. People will hesitate to buy from you again if the experience they had during the transaction was unpleasant, even if you offer a product or service that is exclusive to your area or industry.

With this in mind, what follows are several ideas about enhancing your business through your customer list. Since happy customers are quite likely to tell a friend or colleague about your company, they can provide plenty of word-of-mouth marketing, which is the best kind of all.

- Contrary to popular opinion, the customer is *not* always right. There are some bad customers out there who are nothing but trouble, even though you may bend over backwards to try to please them; you're better off not wasting your time. Focus instead of pursuing the majority of customers who have had good experiences with you. It's important to court your happy customers and spend as little time as possible on the troublemakers.

- Learn to treat all of your customers like family, whether that means taking the time to talk with them about their children, or giving them an extra something. If you'd do it for your own family, then you should do it for your good customers.

- Don't be shy about the success you've had with your current roster of customers. Collect all the testimonial letters you've received and either hang samples on the wall of your lobby or waiting area, or copy and assemble them all in a loose-leaf notebook to put in your waiting area.

- You can ensure that a first-time customer returns to you again and again, and refers others to you, by giving them something for free after their first purchase. It can be expected, as in the case of a technician helping a customer make some minor adjustments to a car stereo, or unexpected, like sending a box of chocolates or flowers a week after you've made a major sale to a new customer.

You Are Your Own Best Marketing Tool

Even if your product or service is the best one or only one around for miles, you will lose business if you are not responsive to your own customers. Twenty-four hours a day, no matter where you go or what you do, you are essentially a walking billboard for your business. So make the most of it. Realize that your own role as your business's best marketing tool can be fun and fulfilling at the same time.

When you become the best source of information for consumers, that's when they will become your customers. Sims, a discount clothing retailer, uses as its motto, "An educated consumer is our best customer." Take the time to teach consumers about your business, whether they call on the phone or walk in off the street. And always try to refer customers to other area businesses if you are unable to help them. But first take down their name, address, and phone number, and send them a handwritten note expressing your hope that they found satisfaction, and extend an invitation to do business with you in the future.

Answers to Seven of the Most Commonly Asked Marketing Questions by New Home-Based Publishers

Q: How will I know which ads aren't working for my business?

A: Most businesses ask new prospects where they heard about their company, but frequently people will give the name of a wrong magazine—or one that doesn't even exist. Classify each ad and article with its own department number and track your responses. Then gear your future advertising and publicity plans towards those markets that pull best.

Q: Marketing is my Achilles heel. I know I should do it, but I'm not sure how to go about it. Where should I start?

A: Marketing is a scary thing for many people, but if you spend an uninterrupted period of time each week just on marketing, your business will grow. Either set aside a five-hour period once a week—and hire someone to answer the phone for the afternoon—or set a goal to accomplish one marketing task each day. For instance, send out letters to five people who have just become new customers to thank them, or send notes and information to five different editors, writers, or producers.

Q: I think my business appeals mostly to women. How do I target them?

A: Gear your promotional material towards the market you want to reach. Then market your business towards two audiences: the general and the specific. General marketing will reach members of your desired audience who don't read specialized publications. The specific markets are smaller, but in most cases, they're more responsive to your message. And the fact that you're marketing towards women has a real benefit: One rule in marketing is if you reach the women, the family will follow.

Q: Help! What should I do when the media calls?

A: Drop everything and smile. Treat them like royalty while you make it appear like it's business as usual.

Q: How do I set my marketing budget as a percentage of total sales?

A: Customarily, businesses should set aside anywhere from 5 to 25 percent of gross sales to invest in marketing and promotion. For home-based publishers who are just getting their businesses off the ground, however, even 5 percent can be too much. Instead, you should put the bulk of your limited energies and dollars into creative, inexpensive marketing strategies like publicity.

Q: How come I see the same books get reviewed in the big magazines over and over again?

A: The publishers of these books spend a good deal of time cultivating their media contacts. Even if a reporter just calls for a brochure, the person in charge of marketing adds them to the media list and regularly sends out personalized notes about new features or programs that concern the publication or company.

Q: Can I really negotiate for better ad rates off the rate card?

A: Yes, especially if the issue closing date is nearing and there's still empty space to fill. Ask the ad director for special rates for new advertisers, frequency discounts, cheaper special sections, and if you can delay your payment until the issue goes to press. It is possible to save up to 75 percent on advertising. Most people simply don't ask, and end up paying full price.

Ten Other Ways to Market Your Business

1. To promote your newest publication, personally deliver a compelling and related object to your most desired media contacts. For example, for the cookbook for working mothers, you can deliver a sample of one of your dishes made from a recipe in the book.

2. If it's appropriate, try to get your product featured as a prize on a local or national game show. This is an effective and fun way to build exposure for your company.

3. If you have written an article about some aspect of your business that has appeared in a local or national publication, send a copy to your 100 best customers.

4. One overlooked way to get publicity for your business is to call in to a live radio talk show that invites listener feedback. Mention your expertise at the beginning and be sure to make a point or give your opinion, and not just to mention your businesses. Other callers may call in to ask how they can get in touch with you, and the show's producer may invite you back to be a guest on the show.

5. One thing you should do when designing publicity campaigns is to borrow liberally from other industries. For instance, if you produce software, plan a media tour around its release in much the same way a book publisher designs a media tour for its authors.

6. One somewhat risky trick employed by some publicists is to leave off of a press release some unique and tantalizing piece of information. Then, when the publicist calls to follow up on the release, she or he can tell the reporter exactly what was left off, which may be all it takes for the reporter to decide to do a story.

7. One author I know has an extremely effective secret weapon for getting his work written up in the media: an extensive rubber stamp collection. When he sends out press mailings, he stamps the envelopes with an appropriate image, in colored ink.

8. Writing a letter to the editor is a good way to promote your business. You can respond to a recent article, citing your experience with your businesses to underscore the point you're making. Then invite readers to contact you for more information. Many publications will print the name and full address of its editorial writers.

9. Print up Rolodex cards listing your name, address, and other contact information, and send off with your press materials. On the tab, include your area of specialty to enable a reporter to use you as a source in future stories on the topic. You may also choose to hand your Rolodex card out to past, present, and future customers.

10. Whenever you do something new for your business, contact the alumni association at any of the schools you've ever attended.

17

Growth and What's Next . . .

Growing any business today can be a challenge. Though everything you do as a home-based publisher will in some way influence how your business grows, most of the time your thoughts will not be on growth, but on putting out all of the little fires that will pop up each day. If you have any time or energy left at the end of the day to think about growth, it may be along the lines of how to slow it down so that you'll have at least fifteen minutes each day to call your own.

But seriously, growth—or the lack of it—is an issue that every home-based publisher has to face at one time or another. Here I want to address how to deal with the variety of ways that growth will manifest itself in the course of running your home-based publishing business. And if you've gotten this far in your determination to start your business, handling growth will probably turn out to be the least of your troubles.

The Problems of Business Growth

Many home-based publishers feel that of all the business problems to have, those that involve issues of growth are among the easiest to handle. It's not always so, however. Growth usually means increased revenue and business, but it may also mean more work and expenses, as well as more headaches to deal with.

Some home-based publishing businesses will grow at a slow, steady rate of 8 to 10 percent a year. Others will explode after a glowing article—complete with price and contact information—in a large-circulation magazine or newspaper. Which is better? While some prefer slow growth as a way to allow them to learn about the business and grow into it, others say that rapid and/or sudden growth provides them with a real education about running a home-based publishing business, and provides a needed boost to the business when the owner might have otherwise been hesitant about forging ahead. This kick in the pants is sometimes exactly what a home-based publisher needs.

Growth *can* be managed and controlled to some extent. How you do it and whether you do, however, it is up to you. One issue you'll face with a growing business is whether or not to hire employees—or if you already have help, whether you should increase their hours to full-time or hire more workers.

Your home-based publishing business is your baby, and if you're used to doing it all yourself you may find it hard to delegate responsibility to someone else, even if it means more free time for you. Most home-based publishers have difficulty letting go at first, but with time and as you begin to see the high level of the ability of the people you do hire, you will trust them more. Such delegation will leave you with time to turn to other problems in the business that need to be addressed.

Another by-product of growth is what to do with the extra money. Some home-based publishers use it to pay off personal debts, but the IRS will still count these monies as taxable income. It's best to pay off personal debts over time, although some people feel that the savings you'll make in not paying debt interest will more than offset the increased tax you'll have to pay.

Some home-based publishers use the extra money to pay off business debts, such as the mortgage. Though it may feel good to own your own house free and clear, the interest you'll be able to deduct from your mortgage payment each month for your home business office can reduce your tax bill at the end of the year, especially if your business will likely show a larger profit with increased income.

One method that many home-based publishers use to invest the money and keep their profits and therefore their taxes down at the same time is to upgrade office equipment and purchase a new phone system or the latest desktop system each year. This will not only cut your taxes, but you'll be able to streamline your operation and also handle more volume, which will increase your revenue—*and* your profits—so that next year you'll have to do the same thing all over again. Granted, though, it's a nice problem to have. Remember, you will have to show a profit three out of five years if you're operating as a sole proprietorship or partnership, but if you've been growing steadily, this will not be a problem.

Managing Employees for Greatest Efficiency

The art of management once prescribed that a boss or manager should rule with an iron fist. Both employer and employee knew who was in charge. The employee went along with this charade, but more often than not, managed to get away with things whenever possible, did only what was expected, and never anything more.

The opposite philosophy is held by the sensitive manager, soft-pedaling harsh news, coddling employees, and always ready to heap lavish praise at the tiniest accomplishment. Again, employees went along with it, but felt they were never fully trusted or appreciated for their own talents and efforts. And, predictably, product quality and morale suffered.

The ideal management style for a small home-based publishing business is to let employees feel as though they are responsible for the business's success or failure; that is, they treat it as though it were their own. This style is also perfect for home-based publishers who need to delegate, and also because home-based staffers will work very closely with you and therefore tend to very quickly develop a personal relationship with the boss. This type of management may run counter to what many people think being a boss ought to be, but in the end, you'll find that your employees will be happier, more productive, and will also stay with you longer if you learn to trust them.

It's not easy to do this, however. People who feel they have to control their employees in order to get them to work may run into problems with this style of management. However, once you see that your employees will treat your business almost as well as you do, it won't take long for you to become a proponent of this management style and actually begin to adopt it in other areas of your life.

Here's how to do it. Say you need to hire an employee to work twenty hours a week at your company, helping out wherever you happen to need it. First, determine the tasks this employee is best at. Train the employee by going through the typical office tasks, from answering the phone to taking phone orders to printing out a press release on the computer. Assure the employee that she or he can approach you with any questions, no matter how trivial they may seem. Encourage the employee to maintain open communication with you at all times. Your end of the deal is to remain open to all queries and always respond in a patient manner.

Then, once it appears the employee thoroughly understands a certain task, open up another challenge. For instance, if taking phone orders is understood, take the next logical step and allow her or him to enter the information into the computer and send out welcome letters to new customers, perhaps with a handwritten note.

If mistakes are made, call attention to them immediately, and then patiently, and without judgment, explain the best way to do it and *why*. Make sure that it's not just because she or he is doing tasks a bit differently from how you would do them. In fact, for maximum efficiency, try not to get too caught up with *how* things get done, rather, that they *do* get done. If you insist that your employees follow certain steps in order to reach the final solution, you'll be trying to squeeze a lot of round pegs into square holes. The outcome may turn out the same, but morale will probably suffer, and your office efficiency will, undoubtedly, drop.

Then, as your employee's responsibilities grow, increase pay based on performance and give regular bonuses and days off with pay. The idea is make your employee feel personally responsible for the customers' satisfaction, so that your time is freed up to work on other projects without worrying about the business.

The secret to successfully managing employees is to show them what to do, trust that they'll do it, and then leave them alone. Though many employees will be taken aback by this unique approach, and some will find it to be too alien for their tastes, the great majority will meet the challenge and help to build your business while cultivating a personal relationship with you.

Some home-based publishers are perfectionists, however, and they think that no one but themselves knows how to do things the right way. Unfortunately, this kind of manager will find it hard to keep employees, and may be burned out by the end of the first year of business.

Compromise and acceptance is the name of the game when it comes to managing employees and maintaining the steady growth of your home-based publishing business.

Secrets of Success

In my opinion, along with many other home-based publishers nationwide, the number one key to success in the industry is through marketing. In this instance, I use the term *marketing* quite loosely: not only does it encompass all of the traditional channels, like advertising and publicity, but it also includes your own personal public relations campaign, or how you interact with your public, that is, your guests.

During every minute that a customer is exposed to your business—either on the phone or through the mail, and with every one of your products—you should be marketing it in a positive light. I'm not talking about the hard sell; after all, they're already customers, and they get plenty of that treatment. The secret of success is to get them to become repeat customers and to tell their friends about the value of your publications. This means being constantly aware of whether or not your home-based business is meeting their needs, and if there's anything more you can do to improve on what you're already doing. However, you should expect that some customers won't welcome this degree of personal interaction with you; in these cases, you'll have to let your products do your marketing for you.

But remember, your marketing job never ends, and that goes for everything you do. If you cease to market, you will soon fade from your customers' memory because it's obvious you didn't care enough about their satisfaction. With thousands of messages bombarding customers each day, you need to stand out to succeed. But that *doesn't* mean a constant hard sell.

Two Typical Problems and Solutions

Though each home-based publishing business will face its own unique set of problems, there are some problems that every entrepreneur will face at one time or another. Here are two of the most common, along with some solutions.

Q: Help! I know I should put money away to help pay the bills when business slows down, but there are always so many other bills that demand my attention that I never seem to get around to it. Also, I'm working so hard that I feel I deserve a reward.

A: Consider putting money aside for your rainy days the same way as you pay your bills. Decide in advance the percentage of your gross deposits that you're going to put into savings, and then do it automatically when you go to the bank.

Ten or twenty percent may not seem like a lot, but it does add up over time. And keep in mind that the reason why many home-based publishing businesses fail is because they don't have enough cash to make it through the downtimes. The owner may decide to take a job in the interim, which will definitely interfere with the ability to keep attracting new customers, that is, if she or he intends to run the publishing business on a full-time basis. So keep stashing it away.

As for rewards, the best kind of treat entrepreneurs can give themselves is some spare time, which doesn't cost anything. So whether you go out for an afternoon or take in a movie, consider the time off to be the best reward.

Q: Running my home-based publishing business keeps me extremely busy, but by the end of the day I look back and I don't seem to have accomplished much. The problem is that the phone rings whenever I'm in the middle of something, or I'm interrupted by something else. What can I do?

A: Learn to make lists, delegate, and take advantage of the quiet times that do occur in the course of each day. Some chronic list-makers, however, regularly put more on their list than they could ever hope to accomplish in a week, let alone a day. If you fall into this category, start by chopping your list in half, or even more. If you manage to check off everything on your list and there's still a few hours in the day, you can always add a few more.

You'll find that you'll get most of your work done in short spurts in between interruptions. Of course, most owners would prefer to have quiet, uninterrupted periods of time all day long, but that's not likely. Make an effort to schedule more uninterrupted periods during the day to allow you to concentrate on your work.

The best way to do this is to let someone else manage the office for you. Have somebody answer the phone for a few afternoons each week—or let the answering machine take the calls. To make sure that you're not interrupted, leave the office and go someplace where you can get some work done. Retreat to a far corner of the house, seek refuge at a friend's house, or even go to the library.

If this is impossible, or if you find you need even more time, take advantage of the quiet times of the day when there are no other demands. If you're not ready to sleep, late night can be a marvelous quiet time to accomplish office or other work.

The trick is to find what works best for you and then stick to it, because it will always be extremely easy to let the day slide into night, working twelve or more hours a day, but with the feeling that you got absolutely nothing done.

Reality Check

All home-based publishers have experienced a time when they were so busy, or so involved with their business, that they learned to completely tune out the world, not venturing beyond the office except to go grocery shopping. Some even get other people to perform these outside tasks for them.

If you're used to commuting to an office every day, you should be prepared for a shock, because you'll have to motivate yourself, and there will be no one else around to do it. In addition, the constant interruptions and lack of personal time can quickly begin to skew your perspective on life and the world. And even if you have regular contact with lots of people over the phone, it's entirely possible that your attitude will begin to change for the worse if you don't venture out at least a few times a week.

That's why it's imperative to get away from the business for a full afternoon or evening at least once a week. Or take one day off every week. Do something that has nothing to do with your business. Do something for yourself for an extended period of time, or else you'll need to refer to the next section a little sooner than necessary.

When to Quit

Burnout and boredom with their subject are the major reasons why home-based publishers decide to sell or close down their businesses. It's so very easy to become caught up in running your business—after all, you are actually giving a performance of sorts to your customers, and all that attention and praise can be very gratifying to the ego—you may reach the point where you have no desire to do anything else. When this happens, you'll know that burnout is soon to come.

Another reason why home-based publishers decide to get out of the business is related to burnout: Running a successful home-based publishing business—or an unsuccessful one, for that matter—is a lot more difficult than it first appears. Many people underestimate the amount of work and overestimate the money that the business will generate—especially the money they think will be available for their own personal use.

You'll know it's time to quit when:

- You no longer become excited about a new development in your topic.
- You can't remember the last vacation you took.
- You work through the holidays.
- You can't remember the last time you woke up feeling refreshed.
- You're so burned out you've lost your enthusiasm for most things.

Of course, home-based publishers who still love what they're doing may feel one or all of these symptoms at one time or another. But when you *honestly* believe the disadvantages of running your home-based publishing business outweigh the advantages, you'll know it's time to quit.

If you decide to opt out of home-based publishing, you should consider selling your business to someone who's new to the field. ("Remember when we were that enthusiastic?" you may say.) Like many home-based publishers, I left the business only to return a few years later.

So take heed—once you start, you may not be able to stop. After all, that ink will get in your blood.

Appendix 1
Sample Business Plan

Litterature
Williams Hill Publishing
Grafton, New Hampshire 03240
A Business Plan by Lisa Shaw

Statement of Purpose

Litterature is a company that produces greeting cards for cats and dogs and for the people in their lives. It is operated as a division of Williams Hill Publishing in Grafton, New Hampshire, a company that has published newsletters, produced software, and currently publishes books about New England and conducts publicity campaigns for other small businesses. This business plan will serve as a blueprint to steer the focus of the company after the first quarter of business, and to offer projections for the first two full years of business.

Section One: The Business

Description of the Business

Litterature is a company that produces greeting cards designed to be sent from people to pets, pets to people, and pets to pets.

Fully three-quarters of the cards currently available can also be used by people to send to other people. Litterature was launched with 101 different cards in quantities of 500 each through a 28-page catalog that serves both wholesale markets and direct sales to consumers. Each card retails for $2.00 and wholesales for $1.00. To serve the wholesale markets, display cards to place in each pocket of a greeting card rack—i.e., Dog Birthday, or Cat Sympathy—were also created, in addition to a topper with the company name to place atop each rack. A graphic designer was hired to scan each card, clean it up for the printer, and then set it to film, in addition to laying out and designing the catalog, rack cards, and toppers. This layout was then transferred to a Web page with a URL of www.litterature.com.

In addition to the greeting cards, Litterature produces and sells other pet-related objects, including books, party kits, personalized Christmas stockings, mugs, T-shirts, writing kits (a rubber-stamp paw print and ink pad), and other products that enhance and supplement the greeting cards in the wholesale and retail markets. Future products include more varieties of cards, wrapping paper, gift enclosures, gift baskets, customized cards and rolls of perforated postcards for pet professionals, and fund-raising jewelry for humane societies, plus a line of books about cats and dogs.

Litterature utilizes antique postcards as the basis of the art for the cards in order to keep production costs down. The postcards are in the public domain, copyright-free, and cost much less to produce than hiring an artist to create original art. The categories include adoption, birth announcements, happy birthday, happy holidays, good cat/dog, congratulations, missing you, humorous, sorry, get well soon, sympathy (so far, our biggest seller), blank cards, thank you cards to send to pet professionals, and practice-building cards that vets, groomers, and pet sitters can send to their clients.

A strong selling point of the cards is that they will be produced on recycled paper and that 10 percent of the revenues generated by Litterature will be donated to humane societies and other animal welfare associations.

Description of the Market

Studies report that there are approximately seventy million dogs and seventy million cats kept as pets in the United States today. In talking with cat and dog owners on the Internet and in person, I've discovered that many of them already send greeting cards to their pets, except that they have to alter cards for people so that they more accurately represent the purpose of the card. Indeed, a study conducted by the American Animal Hospital Association in 1996 found that 62 percent of pet owners sign a letter or card to be sent to another person or pet, 50 percent of pet owners celebrate their pet's birthday, and 79 percent of pet owners give their pet a present for their birthday and for the holidays.

Litterature currently pursues customers in the following areas:

- Publicity in pet-oriented publications as well as mainstream media.
- Appearances at trade shows, pet shows, and crafts fairs with booth rentals.
- Co-op marketing with other pet-related small businesses, i.e., providing a catalog for the manufacturer of Video Catnip or the manufacturer of Vermont Animal Cookies to enclose when they fulfill an order.
- Direct marketing to selected rented lists, both trade and consumer.
- Marketing with a Web page and links to other dog and cat Web pages.
- Wholesaling to gift shops, pet shops, bookstores, and catalog companies that sell pet products through our present network of fifty reps in New England, the Midwest, the Pacific Northwest, California and the Southwest, and North and South Carolina.

- Bulk single-card sales to vets, kennels, and other feline care professionals.

Description of the Competition

There are literally thousands of greeting cards with cats on them, but most are designed to be given to humans, not cats.

There are a handful of companies producing greeting cards for cats or dogs, but they fall into one of two categories: They are either small part-time crafts businesses with a line of ten to twenty cards, or they are a line extension of a huge corporation like Hallmark or American Greetings. Indeed, in a recent article in the *Boston Globe* on December 9, 1996, lifestyle columnist Diane White devoted her column to the topic of greeting cards for pets: "Have Fido and Fluffy Sent Out All Their Greeting Cards?" (Carlton Cards produces 50 different cards, while Hallmark publishes 97 different cards. We beat both of them by producing 101 different cards with our first line). And this was the second time in one month that Litterature was written up in the *Globe;* the first article, "Next Time Rover Scares a Postman, Just Hide His Mail," appeared in the Sunday, November 3, 1996, New Hampshire Weekly edition of the paper.

Litterature is the first large-scale company producing greeting cards for cats and dogs on both a domestic and international basis.

Description of the Management

Lisa Shaw has served as publisher and editor at Williams Hill Publishing, which has produced two successful newsletters— *Sticks* and *Travel Marketing Bulletin*—and a computer software program entitled *The Business Traveler's Guide to Inns and B&Bs.* She has also written twenty books for other publishers, two of which are cat books: *The Quotable Cat,* published in 1992 by Contemporary Books, and *The Cat on My Shoulder,* a book about famous writers and their cats, published in hardcover by

Longmeadow Press in 1992 and brought out in paperback by Avon in 1993.

She has conducted marketing and publicity campaigns for other publishers, and her efforts for Williams Hill Publishing have resulted in editorial mentions in the *Wall Street Journal, USA Today, New York Magazine, Self Magazine, Playboy,* the Associated Press national newswire, and many other national publications.

She will continue to write books for other publishers and to conduct publicity campaigns for other small businesses to generate revenue to help to build Litterature.

Description of the Personnel

Williams Hill Publishing will continue its tradition of farming out extra work to independent contractors and small businesses that specialize in the services that Litterature will require. An 800-number order-taking service is already in place, orders are packed in-house, and a local printer produced the cards, envelopes, catalogs, rack cards, and toppers.

For the first year, I expect not to hire any employees. I should be able to handle rep management as well as continuing to fulfill orders in-house. Should this start to consume too much time, I will contract an outside fulfillment company to pack and ship wholesale and retail orders.

Marketing Efforts

The early marketing efforts at Litterature have been extensive. They include the following:

- Media publicity to encourage direct sales to consumers, help reps present the line with credibility, and increase visibility to retailers and other wholesale markets. Press clippings are attached and include the *Wall Street Journal,* several major-market drive-time radio station interviews (Chicago; St.

Louis, which brought over 200 inquiries from a five-minute interview; Toledo), hundreds of appearances in newspapers all across the country (complete with 800 number and ordering information) from the *San Francisco Chronicle* to the *Nashville Tennessean* to the *Chicago Tribune*. Magazines that have mentioned the cards include *Family Circle, TWA Ambassador, Publishers Weekly,* and *Cats Magazine*. TV shows that have mentioned the cards include *The Tonight Show, The Fox News Channel,* and TNN's *Prime Time Country.*

- Specialized mailings to 200 sales reps and rep groups in the gift and pet markets. This mailing has resulted in the signing of 50 different reps all across the country, including the West, which I believe is the area of the country that will become the largest customer base for Litterature and its products.

- Trade show exhibits at two major pet industry shows in the fall (H. H. Backer Christmas Show in Chicago in October 1996; World Wide Pet Supply Association Northern California trade show in San Francisco in November 1996) exposed the Litterature line to pet shop owners, veterinarians, groomers, and the pet industry media. The article about Litterature that appeared in the February issue of *Cats Magazine* was a direct result of meeting the magazine's editor at the Backer show.

- Direct mailings to catalogs that feature cat and dog merchandise. Nothing solid yet, but many of our reps sell to catalogs, so the repetition factor should help here.

- Direct mailings to the owners of pet cemeteries.

- Direct mailings to other pet manufacturers for co-op marketing projects and bulk premium sales.

- Direct mailings to veterinarians in New Hampshire, Vermont, and Maine increased exposure of the cards. Our regional sales reps visit veterinarians on their rounds and are regularly met with name recognition.

- Links to our Web site from other pet-related Web pages. So far, Internet orders are slowly trickling in, about one a week, but having a Web site definitely caters to the impatient among us who don't want to wait a few days to receive a print catalog in the mail.

- Advertisements in trade publications, such as *Publishers Weekly.* Bookstores are turning out to be a great market for the cards, with the Dartmouth Bookstore in Hanover, New Hampshire, and The Tattered Cover in Denver, Colorado, making wholesale purchases in December 1996.

Marketing efforts in all areas will continue to grow throughout the first two years and beyond. Future marketing plans include focusing on specific groups: dog and cat clubs, shelter fund-raising programs, trade show exhibits at veterinary and grooming conferences, and primarily increasing the wholesale avenues for Litterature.

Summary

Williams Hill Publishing expects that Litterature will be a thriving business within two years, with 100 sales reps and distributors increasing the reach of the greeting cards into the retail market. Once direct sales have been established, Litterature will spend time focusing on bulk markets like vets and kennels, who will become the financial backbone of the company.

In 1997, Litterature will also begin producing its own line of cat and dog books, which will be distributed direct to its own customer list and through wholesale reps to bookstores, pet shops, and gift markets. Litterature's umbrella company, Williams Hill Publishing, will also introduce its first line of books on New England topics in March 1997, beginning with *New Hampshire vs. Vermont,* to be followed by *Free New England,* a guide to free and inexpensive events and attractions throughout the region, scheduled for publication in the spring of 1998. The first two titles from Litterature are planned: *Innside the Animal House: A Guide to Cats & Dogs at New England's Inns & B&Bs,* and a guide to starting and running a pet-oriented business.

The company also has a regional pet magazine on the drawing board entitled *New England Pet,* a monthly tabloid publication that would be solely supported by advertising and distributed free in pet shops, veterinarian offices and groomer shops, bookstores, and other pet-related venues throughout New England. This publication would help to promote Litterature products and help to forge strong relationships with other businesses in the pet industry.

Section Two: Financial Data

Expected Use of Initial Investment

Williams Hill Publishing has invested $33,925 from March 1996 through January 1997.

$12,500	Printing of 101 card designs, 500 of each card and envelope
$6,000	Printing of 15,000 catalogs
$4,085	Printing of rack display and topper cards
$5,000	Booth rental and travel expenses to display at two trade shows
$1,000	Postage
$1,500	Phone expenses
$840	Copier rental for six months
$3,000	Miscellaneous expenses
$33,925	

Williams Hill Publishing expects that once the network of sales reps becomes fully operational in February 1997, it will take three to four months until regular revenue from wholesale accounts is being generated. We plan to add reps until the entire country is covered; we've acquired fifty reps in twenty-five states in just two months. The minimum wholesale order is $150, with 20 percent paid to the reps as a wholesale commission; wholesale accounts pay for all shipping expenses.

Projected revenue is as follows and is admittedly conservative:

If each of forty-five reps sells two Litterature orders each month, the monthly gross revenue will be $13,500 (45 × 2 × $150). The rep commission paid out will be $2,700, which leaves $10,800. These revenues should be generated by April or May. Since I plan to double the number of Litterature reps across the country by the end of 1997, for a total of ninety reps, the revenues cited here will double: monthly gross will be $27,000 (90 × 2 × $150 each), with rep commissions totaling $5,400.

Projected sales from consumer markets as well as specialty markets—i.e., premium sales, bulk and rack sales to vets—will contribute to the revenue stream, but compared to wholesale revenue, it represents 10 to 15 percent of gross revenue; I view this market as primarily serving to increase exposure of Litterature to the general public. In addition, I hope to be able to phase out direct sales to consumers within twelve to eighteen months, after the rep network is able to saturate the retail market with greeting cards and our other products.

Williams Hill Publishing expects first-year revenues of $45,000, with most of that figure generated through wholesale markets. This includes sales of our books and other ancillary products, like Christmas stockings, birthday party kits, and feline and canine writing kits, as well as direct sales to consumers and bulk sales to pet professionals.

Appendix 2
Sample Marketing Plan

Marketing Plan for Litterature

Williams Hill Publishing expects that approximately 20 percent of the annual revenues generated by Litterature will be spent on marketing in the first year. We project first-year revenues at $45,000, with most of that figure generated through direct sales. Sales of books and other ancillary products—such as Christmas stocking packages for cats—will add another $5,000 to the total.

Litterature will really expand in 1997, riding on a wave of positive publicity and inquiries from sales reps and distributors so that wholesale revenues will begin to take hold, as well as bulk sales to vets and kennels.

The four major methods of marketing are detailed in the business plan. What follows is a month-by-month marketing plan:

First month: Mail press kit, catalogs, and sample cards to 400 media names. One week later, make follow-up calls.

> Approximate cost, including printing, postage, phone calls, and labor: $600

Also, send catalog and sample cards to self-generated in-house mailing list, open a Litterature Web page and provide links to and make announcements on other cat-related Internet sites.
Approximate cost: $300

Second month: Visit local shops to sell selected cards. Provide them with racks and set up accounts.

Approximate cost: $200

Third month: Book a booth at two major cat shows, one in New England and one in the New York metropolitan area.

Booth rentals: $500
Travel expenses: $500
Total: $1,000

Fourth month: Rent a partial—5,000 names—list of veterinarians. Prepare a simple letter inviting them to set up an account—paid by check or credit card, to simplify bookkeeping and provide immediate cash—to purchase single-topic greeting cards they can send to their clients. Check results before mailing to larger list.

Mailing list rental: $250 ($50 per 1,000 names)
Printing: $1,400
Postage: $1,000 (Bulk rate at local mailing house)
Handling: $200 ($40 per 1,000 pieces)
Total: $2,850

Fifth month: Rent a partial—5,000 names—list of kennels and groomers. Prepare a simple letter inviting them to set up an account—paid by check or credit card, to simplify bookkeeping and provide immediate cash—to purchase single-topic greeting cards they can send to their clients. Check results before mailing to larger list.

Mailing list rental: $250 ($50 per 1,000 names)
Printing: $1,400
Postage: $1,000 (Bulk rate at local mailing house)

Handling: $200 ($40 per 1,000 pieces)
Total: $2,850

Sixth month: Take time to tabulate figures to see which marketing effort performed best.

Cost: $0

Seventh month: Do another press mailing again to the original media list of 400 names plus 100 new names to be targeted. This time, include press clippings from media who have already mentioned Litterature, and alert them to upcoming press appearances as well.

Approximate cost: $750

Ninth month: Make follow-up calls for the press mailing.

Approximate cost: $100

Tenth month: Book a booth at two major cat shows, one in New England and one in the New York metropolitan area. This time, frame your press clippings and display them at your booth.

Booth rentals: $500
Travel expenses: $500
Total: $1,000

Eleventh month: Arrange with as many catalogs and mail-order retailers as possible to enclose a Litterature catalog whenever they fill an order. Provide them with catalogs and pay them 25 cents for each catalog they send.

Approximate cost: $300

Twelfth month: Again take stock of which marketing effort worked best in the last year. Call your best customers and ask for feedback about future projects. Draw up your marketing plan for next year.

Approximate cost: $100 (for phone calls)

Total annual marketing expenses: $10,500

Resources

Booklets

"How to Write and Market Booklets for Ca$h"

Paulette Ensign

Eighty-page blueprint of how she sold over 400,000 copies in two languages of a 16-page tips booklet, all without spending a penny on advertising.

$35.00, shipping included

"110 Ideas for Organizing Your Business Life"

Paulette Ensign

Sixteen-page tips booklet that includes information on paper, time, and space management.

$5.00, shipping included

Tips Products International, a division of Organizing Solutions, Inc.

Web site: http://www.realvoices.com/booklets

E-mail: booklets@realvoices.com

Phone: 619-481-0890

Fax: 619-793-0880

12675 Camino Mira Del Mar, #179

San Diego, CA 92130

Books

Specialty Booksellers Directory
Ballou, Kiefer, and Kremer
Ad-Lib Publications, $19.95
51 North Fifth Street
Fairfield, IA 52556

The Prepublishing Handbook
Patricia J. Bell
Cat's-paw Press, $12.00
9561 Woodridge Circle
Eden Prairie, MN 55347

How to Become a Bestselling Author
Stanley J. Corwin
Writer's Digest Books, $14.95

Publicity for Books and Authors
Peggy Glenn
Aames-Allen Publishing; $16.95 (hardcover), $12.95 (paperback)
924 Main Street
Huntington Beach, CA 92648

The Huenefeld Guide to Book Publishing
John Huenefeld
Mills & Sanderson Publishers, $29.95

Book Publishing Resource Guide
Marie Kiefer
Ad-Lib Publications, $25.00
51 North Fifth Street
Fairfield, IA 52556

Book Marketing Made Easier
John Kremer
Ad-Lib Publications, $14.95
51 North Fifth Street
Fairfield, IA 52556

Directory of Book, Catalog, and Magazine Printers, 4th Edition
John Kremer
Ad-Lib Publications, $15.00
51 North Fifth Street
Fairfield, IA 52556

1001 Ways to Market Your Books
John Kremer
Ad-Lib Publications, $19.95
51 North Fifth Street
Fairfield, IA 52556

Self-Publishing, Self-Taught
Peter McWilliams
Prelude Press, $20.00
8159 Santa Monica Boulevard
Los Angeles, CA 90046

The Self-Publishing Manual
Dan Poynter
Para Publishing, $19.95
P.O. Box 2206
Santa Barbara, CA 93118-2206

The Complete Guide to Self-Publishing
Tom and Marilyn Ross
Writer's Digest Books, $18.95

1001 Ways to Market Yourself and Your Small Business
Lisa Shaw
Perigee Books, $12.95

Newsletters

Book Marketing Update: Newsletter
John Kremer
Ad-Lib Publications, $60.00 annual subscription
51 North Fifth Street
Fairfield, IA 52556

Organizations

Publishers Marketing Association
2401 Pacific Coast Highway, Suite 102
Hermosa Beach, CA 90254
Phone: 310-372-2732

Index

A

Accountant, determining need for, 104

Accounting basics for home-based publishing business, 110–11

Accrual accounting, 111

Advantages of home-based publishing business. *See also* Disadvantages of home-based publishing business

  for booklets, 31

  for books, 39

  for greeting cards, 48

  for magazines, 55

  for newsletters, 61, 64

  for newspapers, 69, 70

  for software, 73

  for zines, 77

Advertisements

  described in business plan, 209

  learning about nonworking, 189

Advertising

  bartering, 79

  on budget, 176–79

  designed in marketing plan, 171

  determining rate of return on, 175–76

  to gain consumer awareness, 177

  geared for people over fifty, 58

  limitations of, 176

  in magazines, 178

  marketing as distinct from, 167, 174

  newsletters as generally not accepting, 64

  for newspapers, 70, 72, 178

  outside sales staff for, 55

  overreliance on, 176–77

  saving money in, 33–36, 178–79, 190

Advisory board for new projects, drawing on, 151–52

Alumni association of your past schools to publicize business, 192

America Online, working at home forums of, 164

Animals in home office, 159–60

Answering machine

  and faxes, 124

  phone with built-in, 122–23

Assets and liabilities, assessing, 22–23

Association members, newsletters published to inform, 63

AT&T

  home office system by, 128–29

  picturephone by, 133

Attitude for running home-based publishing business, 21

Attorney, determining need for, 103–4

Audience

  defining target, 170

  marketing toward target, 189–90

  providing service to, 15

  response to unsolicited endorsement of, 180

  size of, 15

  slanting story for, 56

  specialized newspapers for specific, 70

  for zines, 79–80

199 Great Home Businesses You Can Start (and Succeed in) for Under $1,000

How to Choose the Best Home Business for You Based on Your Personality Type

Tyler G. Hicks

ISBN 1-55958-224-3 / paperback / 288 pages
U.S. $12.95 / Can. $18.95

This step-by-step guide from bestselling home-based business guru Tyler Hicks shows how you can free yourself from the uncertainties of the job market and go into business for yourself—without going into debt. You'll find all the essential details you need to select and launch the perfect home business for you, whether it's as an import/export entrepreneur, a computer service provider, a wedding planner, or any

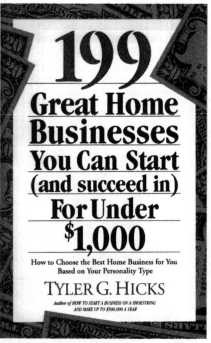

of dozens of other possibilities—all for start-up costs of next to nothing to less than $1,000. You'll soon be your own boss in a lucrative, dependable career with these surefire strategies.

Visit us online at www.primapublishing.com

101 Best Home-Based Businesses for Women

Everything You Need to Know About Getting Started on the Road to Success

Priscilla Y. Huff

ISBN 0-55958-703-2 / paperback / 368 pages
U.S. $12.95 / Can. $18.95

This savvy guide tells you everything you need to know to successfully start and run your own business from the comfort and convenience of your home. Learn how to choose the home-based business that's perfect for you. Understand the first steps of every successful business. Find and use valuable resources to create the job you love. For each of the 101 businesses featured here—from catering to tax preparation and beyond—you'll find valuable information about start-up costs, financing, customer profiles, marketing strategies, and income potential, along with loads of inspiration and helpful business tips tailored to women.

Twice As Many Women As Men Are Starting New Businesses. Here's How They're Making It and How You Can, Too!

101 *Best* HOME-BASED BUSINESSES FOR *Women*

Everything You Need to Know About Getting Started on the Road to Success

PRISCILLA Y. HUFF

Visit us online at www.primapublishing.com

To Order Books

Please send me the following items:

Quantity	Title	Unit Price	Total
_____	199 Great Home Businesses You Can Start (and Succeed in) for Under $1,000	$ 12.95	$ _____
_____	101 Best Home-Based Businesses for Women	$ 12.95	$ _____
_____	_____	$ _____	$ _____
_____	_____	$ _____	$ _____
_____	_____	$ _____	$ _____

Subtotal	$ _____
Deduct 10% when ordering 3-5 books	$ _____
7.25% Sales Tax (CA only)	$ _____
8.25% Sales Tax (TN only)	$ _____
5.0% Sales Tax (MD and IN only)	$ _____
7.0% G.S.T. Tax (Canada only)	$ _____
Shipping and Handling*	$ _____
Total Order	$ _____

*Shipping and Handling depend on Subtotal.

Subtotal	Shipping/Handling
$0.00–$14.99	$3.00
$15.00–$29.99	$4.00
$30.00–$49.99	$6.00
$50.00–$99.99	$10.00
$100.00–$199.99	$13.50
$200.00+	Call for Quote

Foreign and all Priority Request orders:
Call Order Entry department
for price quote at 916-632-4400

This chart represents the total retail price of books only (before applicable discounts are taken).

By Telephone: With MC or Visa, call 800-632-8676 or 916-632-4400.
Mon–Fri, 8:30-4:30.

WWW: www.primapublishing.com

By Internet E-mail: sales@primapub.com

By Mail: Just fill out the information below and send with your remittance to:

Prima Publishing
P.O. Box 1260BK
Rocklin, CA 95677

My name is _____

I live at _____

City _____ State _____ ZIP_____

MC/Visa#_____ Exp. _____

Check/money order enclosed for $_____ Payable to Prima Publishing

Daytime telephone _____

Signature _____